*Holy a*

# Holy and Unholy Ghosts

A Priest's Experience of the Supernatural

## by Peter Mullen

Thorsons
*An Imprint of HarperCollinsPublishers*

Thorsons
An Imprint of HarperCollins*Publishers*
77–85 Fulham Palace Road
Hammersmith, London W6 8JB
1160 Battery Street
San Francisco, California 94111–1213

Published by Thorsons 1995
10   9   8   7   6   5   4   3   2   1

A catalogue record for this book
is available from the British Library

ISBN 1 85538 479 5

Printed in Great Britain by
HarperCollinsManufacturing Glasgow

To Karl

# Contents

# Introduction

### What are these things, ghosts, anyway?

Last summer we were driving through a thunderstorm across the remote North Yorkshire moors when my son Tom, aged 14, announced – rather bravely, I thought, in the circumstances – 'I don't believe in ghosts, or anything like that.' An hour's fascinating conversation followed.

Tom's statement sounds reasonable enough, but what does it mean? It turned out that he meant to say that he didn't believe that ghosts are supernatural manifestations of those who have died. 'Why not?' I asked. He gave a me long answer to this question, the gist of which was that he simply didn't believe that there is such a realm as the supernatural. End of argument.

Except that I persisted.

'Why do you say there is no such thing as the supernatural when so many people claim to have had experience of it?'

He said, 'I think people make up these stories about ghosts.'

'OK – let's assume that nine out of ten of all the people who tell of their ghostly experiences are born liars. That still leaves ten per cent who are telling the truth.'

'They're mistaken,' he said.

I tried to reason that all arguments are based on the weighing of probabilities and that it is extremely improbable that all reports of ghosts can be dismissed as either lies or errors.

'Let's suppose,' I said, 'that just one case in 1,000 is neither a lie nor a mistake – then what?'

We drove on in silence for a long time after that.

Finally, I said, 'Well, I've seen a ghost. Are you calling me a liar?'

He said, 'No. I think you were mistaken.'

What was the nature of my 'mistake'? I thought I saw my dead grandmother at the bottom of my bed one night. I was convinced it was no trick of the light nor something brought on by an attack of indigestion. The apparition looked just like my grandma, moved like my grandma; but my grandma was dead. What else could I say to describe my experience accurately except that I genuinely believed I had seen her ghost?

We live in a scientific age, or so we say. I think rather that we live in a pseudo-scientific age, a materialistic age in which we are inclined to dismiss automatically any phenomenon which does not conform to materialistic expectations. It is often said that the religious age was an era of primitive superstition and prejudice. But it seems to me that the modern age has not given up being prejudiced; we have merely exchanged one set of prejudices for another.

For example, there is nothing in logical thought to say that there cannot be such things as ghosts. Spiritual manifestations can be denied only if we first declare that there is no such thing as a spiritual realm – if, that is, we adopt a prejudice in favour of materialism. Such a prejudice is still a prejudice, even when we try to glorify it by calling it *scientific*.

Actually, there is a strong scientific argument in favour of the existence of ghosts. It is the business of science not to rule out in advance any explanation for particular phenomena. If, therefore, I am convinced that I have seen my grandma, but my grandma is dead, then one possible explanation is that I have in fact seen her ghost. That explanation can only be ruled out completely by someone who is absolutely prejudiced in favour of materialism as the *only* explanation for *everything*.

Most of the world's religions claim that there is more to creation than what is physically apparent. This life is regarded as a part of a greater life sometimes described as 'eternity' – something for which life in the here and now is a preparation. If we can suspend the materialist prejudice for a moment, then we may admit that the other world, the world of eternity, might sometimes break into this world, and that when this happens we see ghosts.

Moreover, the great religions teach that experience is not all of a piece. Some experiences are more significant than others. You do not have to be religious to accept this. Experiences and feelings of deep love or lasting hatred or fear run very deep in all of us and they are different in quality from ordinary experiences of, say, merely feeling a bit hungry or a bit bored. If there is a spiritual realm beyond this one, then we might expect that places and occasions which have been full of powerful feelings might, as it were, leave traces in the physical world.

Perhaps this is why so many ghost stories are filled with high emotions? We read of ghostly appearances at locations where profound emotions were expressed: the house in which a murder took place; the scene of tragic love; the site of deep and unfulfilled longing. It is as if there is some unfinished business. Indeed, a charged atmosphere at such places is exactly what anyone – except someone hidebound by materialist prejudice – would expect.

But ghosts may be explained even in materialistic terms. Modern science is not like ancient science. In the older way of looking at the world, matter was regarded as being composed of millions of tiny pieces, particles or atoms. These were thought to be just like bits of dust, only infinitesimally small. Modern science – particularly the theories of quantum mechanics – has come to regard matter as a vast interrelated system of electrical charges. To put it crudely, matter is nowadays seen as a lot less material than it used to be.

Ghostly appearances, then, may be a special sort of physical manifestation – matter in another form. Such a thing is possible. In its brief history, science has already discovered one strange force or medium that would have been totally incomprehensible to our forefathers: radio waves. These can make images appear at great distances through the television screen in our own front rooms. What is thereby created is an illusion, a picture. It is not itself a reality, but it is a real representation of reality. That war in Africa is really being fought; the Test Match in Australia is at this moment being played.

We do not see these things *really*, yet we do see them; and what we are seeing *is real*.

Ghostly appearances may therefore be by means of a force in the universe as yet undiscovered in its precise working but similar to radio waves. It really would be a sign of arrogance and prejudice to claim that no such force could possibly exist: a prejudiced person from the tenth century AD might have said the same about the impossibility of radio and television, *and he would have been wrong.*

## Angels and devils – supernatural visitors?

The Devil gets a very bad press. He is always portrayed as a real 'baddie'. He is the personification of evil and the enemy of God. But he was not originally perceived in this way. In the Bible, in the Book of Job, Satan is the proper name of a spirit who is called 'one of the sons of God'. He has a function and that is to test the sincerity and virtue of men and women who claim to love and serve God. In the case of Job, Satan does his work well.

Satan sees that Job is a very rich man with houses, farms and land and a lovely family. So, one day in the heavenly court, he says to God, 'Job doesn't love you for nothing, but because you've made him wealthy.'

God then gives Satan leave to strip Job of his privileges as a test of his devotion to the godly and virtuous life.

In the biblical thought of this period, Satan is seen as God's counsel for the prosecution. The Devil was not therefore regarded as a sort of equal and opposite of God – a dark or wicked god, eternal and all-powerful like God himself – for that would be to declare the existence of two gods, and this the Bible refuses to do. The Jewish–Christian scriptures are monotheistic. There is only one God; indeed, the first of the Ten Commandments says that humankind must not accept the existence of any other gods.

As the Bible story develops, Satan's character also develops and he comes to be seen as a fallen angel, a disobedient spirit who clutched at equality with God. The last book in the Bible tells how this upstart is eventually put in his place and 'beaten down under our feet'. In the meantime, Satan wreaks his peculiar kind of havoc on Earth and in the hearts of humans by constantly suggesting to us that there is a way to happiness other than the service of God. In the New Testament, he even makes this suggestion to Christ himself in the story which we have come to know as the Temptations in the Wilderness.

Satan is sometimes called Lucifer and the name means 'Bringer of Light'. This underlines the teaching that the Devil is an angel, but a fallen angel whose fall was brought about by his attempt to rival the one true God.

As for angels, the word αγγελos – angelos – is simply the old Greek word for messenger. It was believed that communication existed between this world and the other or heavenly world, and that such communication required intermediaries. These were the angels. They were given wings only by the artistic and cultural fashions of the Middle Ages and the Italian Renaissance. Because we inhabit a physical world, and because we are creatures with senses, we necessarily make pictures and representations of spiritual and psychological realities. This does not mean that *real* angels – if they exist – have wings. But, of course, it does not mean that they *do not* have them either!

Spiritual experiences are nowadays regarded as a good thing in themselves, irrespective of their quality. No doubt this has something to do with the feeling of emptiness which afflicts many people in our secular and materialistic age. It is as if we say to ourselves, '*Any* spiritual experience will do – because it proves that there *must be something*!' We look for a 'little bit of magic' even though we may suspect that the old gods are dead.

So in the materialistic world an account of a misadventure with the ouija board is as notable as a vision of the Virgin Mary – more notable if it is lurid enough. Mind over matter, spoonbending, levitation, spiritual healing, witchcraft or the rumour of it – any or all of these things (sometimes in combination) are welcomed as relief from the intolerable thought that the world is nothing but rational explanations.

It was not always so. Older civilizations distinguished between good and bad spirits. They believed in the supernatural realm but did not maintain that every manifestation of it is necessarily good. In the Western tradition of spirituality, the history of our own civilization, the Bible says, 'Believe not every spirit, but try the spirits whether they are of God' (*I John* 4:1). It is as well to bear this warning in mind.

The truth is that spiritual reality is the highest reality, the most powerful force in the universe. It is not subject to the ordinary rules of mechanics. It can be sublime and all-loving, as in God and Jesus Christ, the angels and archangels. But it can also be evil and destructive. The words 'Devil' and 'demons' are symbols which describe this unwelcome aspect of spiritual experience.

Perhaps you are not inclined to believe in God or the Devil? This book is not an attempt to convert anyone to such belief. It is simply the case that God and the Devil are characters in the spiritual history of humankind: they are part of our story and aspects of our psychological makeup whether we like the fact or not. They may be more than this, of course; perhaps they actually exist as supernatural beings in their own right. Whether they do or not does not matter at all to the reading of these stories. It is simply that when people talk about the supernatural and recount their experiences of it, they use the words and titles 'God', 'the Devil', 'angels' and 'ghosts', etc. So anyone who, like me, fills a book with such stories, is bound to use those words and titles too. I do so without prejudice in favour or against any supernatural reality which may or may not exist, as it were, *behind them*. I am simply using the accepted vocabulary for talking about alleged supernatural experiences. The reader will have his or her own opinions on the precise status of these phenomena.

I am making no claim to know what ghosts are. I am simply saying that these rather unusual experiences have been reported to me in the course of my daily work and that the people who make these reports are neither plain mad nor conspicuous liars. The experiences are fascinating on their own terms, whatever explanation anyone might want to offer about their nature and origin. All I am saying is that they were reported to me in good faith and so I request that anyone reading them does so with an open mind.

*Peter Mullen,*
York, 1995.

# 1

...

# *The mill*

I spent two years as a curate in Oldham, Lancashire, which was once the most famous cotton town in the country. The mills were all closed down by the time I was there in the early 1970s, but the buildings remained, used as warehouses or light engineering factories. Most of the chimneys had gone too, but a few still stood like the artefacts of a previous civilization.

Oldham is up in the Pennines, the damp, windy hills known as the Backbone of England. And cotton was itself woven into the sinews of that north country. When there was a slump the town fell idle and silent and in the boom years it bustled with confidence and gaiety. There were other landmarks as well as the old chimneys: St Mary's Parish Church and, right alongside, Tommy Fields market, bright with fruit and vegetables, where also you could buy the local delicacy of black peas and the celebrated black pudding.

The rows of terraced houses, 'old Oldham', had been demolished and vast new housing developments had gone up in their place –'Legoland', as they were less than affectionately named by the old-timers. Everyone seemed to have something of the old-timer about them and, as the saying went, 'Even the kids are old before they're young.' This is not to suggest that they lacked energy or zest for life – any of them, young or old – only that they were a community with traditions, a people with history.

This tradition was perpetuated in their language, which described the present in terms of the past and its landmarks. If you said, 'Down past Colley's Mill at Chadderton,' for example, everyone knew where that was, though there had not been a Colley's Mill for 30 years.

The curate's flat was a third-floor apartment on the east side of the hill called Oldham Edge. When you ascended this hill on the way home from church or shopping, you knew what 'edge' meant: a gale-blown escarpment looking down distantly to the villages of Delph and Denshaw and away beyond them to bleak, black Saddleworth Moor.

There were disused chimneys in this landscape, like old men's tobacco pipes. One of them was to be demolished, and its mill with it, to make room for a car park. Notices had been posted about the demolition and people were looking forward to seeing it. I had observed the ritual before: children ran about and had to be yelled at to keep clear of the taped-off area; men stood in silence, just looking; women in flowery pinafores watched, interested but wistful – as anyone might witness a great detumescence.

The night before, I slept badly, troubled by loud dreams whose cause I drowsily attributed to the noise of machinery being drawn up to effect the destruction. I seemed to see hordes of working men and women, agitated and distraught, as ropes and pulleys and siege-engines surrounded the chimney. It was one of those frustrating, enervating dreams which never seem to get to the point. The chimney was not pulled down, neither in my dream nor in reality. This I could be certain of in the morning as I saw it through the bathroom window, black against the sky.

It had been the restless sort of night that makes you feel glad to be awake. I spoke to others on my way to church and some of them had also had disturbed sleep. We put it down to the bracing Oldham climate: 'Noisy night again, wasn't it?'

The demolition was scheduled for three o'clock and a crowd gathered on Oldham Edge. They looked as if they were all on a sepia photograph. It was spectacular and rather eerie. We were, I suppose, about half a mile from the action and so the sound of the denouement seemed to occur long after the sight of it. There were calls to see the 'action replay'. Then there was only a cloud of yellow dust and we all went home.

..........

A few days later I went to take Holy Communion to an old lady who lived in one of the terraced houses still remaining, right on top of the Edge by the junior school. Mary Knowles had lived in Oldham all her life and now she lived alone. She was a remarkable story-teller and her words seemed to fall out of her mouth like nuggets, solid images that had the ring of truth.

'Once, during the Great War, a great cloud came over Oldham and we all thought we would be taken up into it. It was silent, like soot. . .' That was the tone of Mary's evocations. She would grab my arm and delay me with another story after I had given her Communion. 'I see everything from up here,' she said fiercely, as if anyone would have dared to doubt her! She could hypnotize you with a stare. I called her – not to her face! – 'the Ancient Marineress'. She had of course worked in the mill, but I did not know it had been the very mill whose chimney had been so recently demolished.

'I want to know,' she said to me now, 'if you're a believer?'
I said I hoped I was a believer.

'Oh I don't mean in Him upstairs, God. We all believe in Him – no choice. I mean, do you believe in the Others?'
The way she said 'Others' – her eyes were like black peas!
'The Others?' I asked weakly.

'The Others,' she repeated, as if talking to a dull child. 'I mean them that's gone on. "Dead" they call 'em. But they're not dead. They were back the other week, the night before Hargreaves chimney was knocked down.

'I'd got up. I knew there was something. I get this feeling – it's always the same. And, out of my window, Hargreaves weaving-shed was all lit again. Bright yellow lights, just like it always used to be. All working again. Goodness, there was such a rattle and a clatter!

'And I could see 'em all. Billy Lambert, George Naylor, Betty Butterworth, Maggie Jackes . . . all of 'em come back afore their mill was done away with altogether. I saw 'em!'

Up there, high on Oldham Edge, in that snug little room with the black-leaded range and the green velvet cover over the dining table, I could not avoid her eyes. And the quiet but penetrating voice, more terrifying because it was so matter-of-fact.

'I see all sorts, you know, young man. I could tell you a thing or two to make your hair curl!'

# 2
....
# *Young men seeing visions*

How immune are atheists from supernatural visitations?

Curates are moved around by bishops as if they were chess pieces. After two years in Oldham, I was asked to go and work in the neighbouring town of Bolton. There was a man on our Parochial Church Council there who, I have to admit, irritated me beyond my patience sometimes. Michael was a computer engineer for a multinational company, which he had joined immediately after gaining a first class honours degree in philosophy from Manchester University. He was a militant intellectual with left wing political persuasions and an atheist. What, then, was he doing on the church council of an Anglican parish?

The answer was social and historical rather than religious. His parents had been connected with the church all their lives – his father was Treasurer of St Peter's and his mother a churchwarden – and Michael had been brought up in the tradition, first as choirboy and then as Head Server at the high altar. He had a beautiful voice and his reading of the Gospel on the great festivals was memorable.

Then he went to university and lost his faith. Except that is not the right way to express what happened: he found his anti-faith, his deep-seated resentment towards religion. No doubt psychotherapists would look to his relationship with his parents. Was his rejection of their religion a way of getting back at them for hurts too deep to receive proper articulation? He had no girlfriends. Was that something to do with it?

His antipathy was not explicit, but subtle and cynical. He returned to the parish after graduation and attended church with his parents. Evensong was what he came to. He would no longer receive the Holy Communion. As you were reading the service he could look at you like the very Devil, as if he were saying, 'You don't really believe this codswallop, do you?'

One day his mother asked me if I would speak to him. 'He's so sullen at home all the time. He says some terrible things about the church. I think he's done too much studying – it's turned his mind.'

I made a point of calling to see him when I knew his parents would be out and I asked about his philosophy course.

'The best thing that ever happened to me,' he said. 'It really helped me get a few things sorted out.'

Had it helped him with his faith? I quoted St Anselm at him: '*Fides quaerens intellectum*' – faith seeking understanding.

'Anselm doesn't register very high on the Richter scale these days, Vicar. In fact the existence of God is a question we can't really make sense of at all when you come to think about it.'

I managed to swallow my resentment at the implication that the existence of God was not one of the questions which I had come to think much about. 'Why not?' I asked testily.

'Well, there are two sorts of knowledge, aren't there? Self-evident and empirical. That means –'

'Yes, I know what "empirical" means. It means going and taking a look.'

'Did you do philosophy, then?'

There was an uncomfortable silence. Then Michael said, 'The existence of God isn't self-evident, because I can always deny it without contradicting myself. And it's not empirical, because we don't know what would constitute "taking a look", as you put it. I mean anything that you said was caused by God might just as easily have a natural cause. So we don't even know how to begin asking whether God exists, let alone proving that he does.'

'Some people say they can detect God's action in their own lives.'

'Good for them!'

Under his hard smile I sensed deep hurt. I suspected he was trying to pick a fight and I really did not think that would do much good, so I tried to make a mild joke: 'Well, at least you haven't given up on God completely – I mean, it's nice to see you at Evensong with your mother and father.'

'You think I'm some sort of hypocrite, eh? That I preach atheism and practise churchgoing.' He rolled the edge of the tablecloth fiercely in his fingers as he spoke.

'I don't think you're any sort of hypocrite, Michael. But why are you being so aggressive?'

'I'm not being aggressive!' he shouted, showing no sign of understanding how angry he appeared to be. 'Religion's a load of crap in a scientific age,' he continued. 'I think people like you should be made to do an honest day's work. I've got my own reasons for coming to church, and they've nothing at all to do with religion.'

'Like the teetotaller visiting the pub, are you? Ah well, I'd better be going about my honest day's work.'

There was not the hint of a smile.

I left and walked back to the Vicarage full of the sense that I had been talking to a young man who was deeply troubled. That precocious, talented youth could not have simply transformed into an arrogant loudmouth and nothing else. His qualities were being obscured by a veneer of intellectual confidence – and deliberate rudeness – which was meant to protect but was thoroughly destructive.

A week or two later I received a phone call early in the morning from Michael's mother to tell me that he had been taken into Bolton General Hospital suffering from a burst appendix. 'I'm beside myself with worry, and so's his father. It's deadly serious. And we've both been out of sorts with him recently. He gets so angry, so militant. I think this is the cause of his illness.'

So much bile that he was bursting with it!

It was a day or two before Michael could receive visitors and he looked knocked out, so wan and weak that it was hard to picture him as the strident young man who had been sounding off with such vehemence not very long before. 'Hello,' he said, in a shadow of his normal voice, and mumbled something about the room being too warm. I mentioned this to the staff nurse and called to see him again after about a week, but he had friends from work by his bed so I left without having had the chance of conversation.

The week after that, I was in church early for the midweek celebration of Holy Communion and was startled when I saw Michael in the sparse congregation. At the proper time he came forward, knelt at the altar rail and received the Sacrament. He looked pale and thin and his cheeks were dark hollows. But there was also a calm look about him, a quiet confidence rather than stridency. He moved comfortably within his own space, at ease.

Afterwards he asked me to hear his confession. I cannot reveal what he said in the confessional, but I am happy to record that when that was done he asked for his name to be put back on the servers' rota for Sunday morning Parish Communion: 'Not to be Head Server, you understand – just on the list to take my turn.'

As we walked together down the church path and out into the traffic, he said: 'You know, I resented them – Mum and Dad – because I thought they had taken away my childhood by their strictness. It was only when I got to university that I discovered other kids had done things I'd never dreamed of, never heard of. I felt I'd been cheated.

'It was the same at work. I realized I was really very inexperienced, naïve. And I felt everyone knew it and they were mocking me for it. I guess I was a bit paranoid. And so angry. So bloody nebulously angry!'

He stopped and faced me in the High Street. Lorries and buses rattled by and he had to shout to make himself heard. 'I saw Him as I was lying there in that side ward. He was there all right, in the doorway by the oxygen cylinders. He just said the one word, "Michael," but it was as if He'd said everything about me, everything that was wrong, and put it all right at the same time. He really appeared you know.'

'Empirical, eh?' I said.

Michael's face was all self-mocking smiles. 'God, I'm an idiot!' he said. And we both stood there laughing. The Bolton shoppers must have thought we were a couple of madmen out for the day.

# 3

## The rocking-chair

When I was being trained for the priesthood, it was the conviction of the hierarchy that the best way to protect its future clergymen from the world, the flesh and the Devil was to remove us to the back of beyond. I spent the first two years of my theological preparation in an eighteenth-century country house in Kent with 50 fellow students or 'ordinands', to use the correct title for a trainee priest.

The setting was magnificent. It was rather like living your life in the middle of a BBC classic serial. The mists of our theological ignorance were accompanied by real mists veiling the broad fields and tall trees. There were cattle and sheep in the fields, visual aids as it were to all those animals in the story of Noah and the beasts in Jesus' parables. There was a thatched pub in the village which had been a favourite haunt of fighter pilots during the Second World War, but we were not allowed to visit it.

Quite how we were supposed one day to spring forth from this secluded and chaperoned existence wise and experienced enough to minister to those suffering from the world's ills remains a mystery to me.

Fifty men shut in a country mansion for eight weeks at a time inevitably became a hothouse of nervous intrigue and sexual frustration. Wives and girlfriends were allowed brief visits only. It is embarrassing now to recall how we ogled these 'occasional' women! It was an unnatural setting for men training not to be monks but secular priests.

It was an age when 'gay' was a word which still meant happy and carefree, and certainly before homosexuals had become evangelical in promoting their cause. There were some affairs, of course, even one or two serious ones, and there were a few exotic types who loved affectation and camp, theatrical gestures. But most sexual activity – and it was not pervasive – was furtive, desperate and sporadic, enveloped in great clouds of guilt and recrimination.

I mention all this because there is a school of thought which claims that ghosts and the occult are 'all sex' – that they are fantasies generated by frustrated sexual desire. Perhaps there is something in this supposition. It may be, though, that the hothouse atmosphere in such a place, because of its tenseness, makes some people more sensitive, more predisposed to experience the supernatural.

After the late evening service of Compline we would gather in one another's rooms and inevitably, from time to time, the conversation got round to ghosts. The house was reckoned to be haunted. It was not so much eerie, however, as unpleasant. Most of us were glad to get away from it. No doubt this was mainly to return to wives and girlfriends, but there was also something nasty about the place itself. One of the ordinands described it as 'unwholesome'.

I said it was eighteenth century, and the oldest part of it was, but there were two extensions: one from the nineteenth century and one which had been completed in the late 1950s. My room was at the top of a flight of stairs which joined the eighteenth and nineteenth-century parts. This was reckoned to be one of the haunted spots.

The apparition was a figure in a cloak or cassock – whether male or female could not be discerned, since it always appeared with its back to the viewer. And it had another characteristic mode of appearing: always on its way up the flight of steps outside my room. Someone would be standing or walking in the nineteenth-century part when they would see the black-cloaked figure walk away from them up the stairs into the eighteenth-century section. By the time you ran up after it, it had vanished.

'Have you ever heard anything, Peter? It's right outside your door.' It is an odd sensation when people stare at you and ask questions like that, late at night under a dim light bulb. I never saw it, but many did and they often told their tale: 'I wasn't frightened exactly. Not running scared, you know. But I felt sick. As if it was something evil.'

Not wholesome.

Part of the unwholesomeness about the place generally was the amount of sickness among the residents, particularly at the start of each term. Some of these minor illnesses were stomach upsets which could be put down to a change of diet or water supply, but not all of them could be explained in this way. There were physical injuries, an amazing crop of them – and always at the beginning of term. Many students had nightmares and claimed these did not occur when they were at home.

Neither I nor my room-mate John looked forward much to the rare occasions when nature called in the night: the lavatories were at the bottom of the ghostly flight of stairs. In the dark, there was something intimidating about the narrow length of that corridor with its noisy floorboards and faded yellow paintwork.

Neither of us ever saw the cloaked figure on the stairs, but it turned out that there was a ghost much closer to us than that. One night John awoke in a panic. He was not the sort to panic – he had been a builder before his college days and was tall and sturdy. He would often laugh when, as he called them, 'the creepy crowd' came round to ask if we had seen the spook yet. Often he would excuse himself from these conversations and lie on his bed reading a big book about the England cricket tours.

But that night he was scared out of his wits and very noisy about it. I switched on the light by my bed and went across to calm him down. He was shaking.

'It was a nightmare. You're OK now.'

'It wasn't. I heard something and then I felt so . . . *ill* inside, I thought I was dying. Thought I was dead already. In hell.'

'What was it like?'

'A horrible creaking noise. Like a machine, regular. But that doesn't describe it. It was the feeling that came with it. You must have heard something. It was really loud.'

But I had heard nothing.

John heard it again twice that term and awoke as before. 'We should mention it to the Chaplain,' I said. But he did not want, as he said, anyone 'to start making a fuss', I think he would have felt embarrassed to talk about it.

He was not troubled again all the next term and we largely forgot about it. The term after that was summer and the nights in the countryside were beautiful; the soft atmosphere calm and full of the scents of flowers. We always slept with the windows wide open. They opened out on to a small balcony which overlooked the lawn and the hills to the north. In June there was always a light over the horizon and once or twice, wakened by birdsong, I stood by the window and watched the dawn.

One night I awoke while it was yet dark. John was sleeping silently. It was a lovely night and I had no thoughts of ghosts, no thoughts of anything in particular – I was just lying there enjoying the quiet. Gradually I became aware of something, something that was slowly coming into view, or even slowly coming into being.

It was a hideous woman with long white hair and a terrible grin. She was in a rocking-chair, moving back and forth. The chair itself was part of the apparition. It was like a life-size chalk sketch on a blackboard. There was no sound, no creaking, despite the movement of the chair. The horrible woman seemed to be looking straight at me with evil intent, as if she were deliberately trying to terrify me.

I was terrified, but worse than the terror was the feeling of nausea. And I vomited. The apparition looked at me with a satisfied leer, as if this was the response she – it? – had been hoping to produce. The noise I had made woke John and he put on the light. The apparition had disappeared.

I washed my counterpane in the basement laundry and we decided not to say anything to the principal or the chaplain unless the apparition appeared again. It did not. 'Strange,' said John 'that you never heard the creaking and I saw nothing the night she appeared.'

We were not, as I said at the beginning, supposed to go in the pub in the village. But, of course, we did go in. Towards the end of our time at the college, the rule was waived and then we would go in two or three evenings a week. It was a pleasant relief to talk to the locals; a change from the heated religious atmosphere of the college.

Among the pipe-smoke and banter of the tap room was an old woman called Edie who drank strong brown ale and was in the habit of seizing visitors and commanding their attention all evening. Her stories were mostly about the life of the village before the First World War and even going back into the nineteenth century.

Edie knew a lot about the old mansion which had become our theological college. 'They do say it's haunted,' she told me in the week before I finally left the college forever. 'There was a young girl in the house – very young by all accounts. She had a lover from the Old Priory and he used to go and visit her at night. The girl's mother heard him on the stairs that led to her room and there was the Devil to pay.

'Anyhow, the girl died. Some said the mother killed her, suffocated her. She *did* die right enough. There was a big funeral and she's buried in the churchyard – 1909, as I recall. Whatever – it was all hushed up.'

# 4
....

## *Angels and archangels*

Louise Fawcett, 'Louie', was 86 when I went as curate to my first parish. She was frail and housebound, but 'frail' in the sense that she had the mental strength of ten men and the tenacity of a limpet! She was so small and thin that she was almost disembodied mind, but friends said she had been quite stout in her younger days. She had been headmistress of a local school.

Louise was high church, what is sometimes called 'Anglocatholic', which is to say that she loved the sorts of churches which held elaborate rituals with processions, candles and incense: 'smells, bells and frilly cottas'. But her faith was deeper than mere appearances. It was so real that it was tangible. For Louie the doctrines of the faith were not abstractions or propositions to which you gave intellectual assent, they were as close to daily life as the morning milk and the grocery van. She seemed to be on nodding terms with angels and archangels and the whole company of heaven. Her whole life was a spiritual brocade. Her spare-time activity for 50 years had been the making and mending of the priests' vestments for the parish church. 'Now,' she complained, 'I can't see well enough to sew.' She had never married, but had a home help and friends coming in and out all day long.

In the parish she was regarded with respect bordering on fear. For she spoke her mind and, like the God she worshipped, was no respecter of persons. Even the clergy were afraid of her fierce piety which seemed to some to challenge their own commitment.

One of my jobs was to take Holy Communion to her house every Wednesday and red letter saint's day. She was particular about the way this should be carried out. Visit some homes with your little black box with the Communion set inside and the bread and wine, and you would be instantly offered tea and treated to a discourse on last night's performance by City or United! But Louie would receive you in silence and she observed strictly the rule which said there should be no secular chat until the sacramental act had been completed.

Her conversation was spiritual rather than 'religious'. I mean, the usual question from house communicants is, 'Were there many in church on Sunday?' But Louie's subject was God. This was not oppressive, for her love of God took the form of a general rejoicing in God's creation.

Too blind to sew or not, she still had an eye for the flowers and trees and for the birds which had visited her lawn that morning. And she made jams and cakes religiously. There was no hint of the puritan in Louie. She was never as shocked as most others of her age (and younger) by the sleazier and less law-abiding elements in local life.

'Most of our sins,' she once said, 'are the result of human folly rather than human wickedness. God will laugh at us on Judgement Day and then what red faces we shall all have!' That was how she talked. She never spoke much about herself.

Louie had written a history of the parish and the Vicar wanted to get this off to the printers so that we might have copies at the back of the church and, not least, so that Louie might see her work in a finished form. But when it came to declaring a piece of work completed, Louie was as diffident, and difficult, as Dr Casaubon brooding over the penultimate draft of his *Key To All Mythologies*. 'I just want to read through the 1940s chapter once more,' she would say. The Vicar had asked me to try to hurry her up a bit.

One winter she had a bad attack of bronchitis and the doctor was coming to see her twice a day at one stage. Louie never complained about feeling unwell, only that her illness was a nuisance in that it prevented her from doing all she wanted to do. The bronchitis did not clear up, even after two courses of antibiotics, and Louie was taken off in an ambulance for further tests and kept in hospital for a week.

I went to see her as usual one Wednesday in late February and she called me to the window to observe all the signs of spring. The illness had knocked her back. She looked so delicate, like a hand-painted figurine in fine china. She was nonetheless very businesslike that morning.

'I want you to look at the last few pages of my parish history with me and then you can take it to Father Michael.'

(Michael Hewlett was the Vicar. Louie called all Anglican clergymen 'Father'.)

The manuscript was beautifully written in her own small handwriting and I could not imagine that anything more could be usefully added to it. Certainly nothing ought further to have delayed its publication.

'That's that, then,' she said. 'I wanted to get that out of the way. I've got cancer, you know. I shan't be here for much longer.'

She explained that they had wanted to keep her in hospital after the tests but she had persuaded them to let her come home to put her affairs in order while she still had the strength. She was prepared to return to hospital when the time came.

In the weeks that followed, I persuaded her to talk about her past a little, for, as I said, 'I feel I know you very well, Louie. But it's odd – I know hardly anything at all *about* you.' So we sat at her window on many afternoons and observed the coming of spring, the slow greening of the bushes, the strengthening light and the daffodils shaking in the wind, in rhythm, as it seemed, with the church bell calling the clergy to Evensong.

Louie was born in 1896 in Kettlewell in the Yorkshire Dales. 'Right by the River Wharfe in its infancy. D'you know, there was never a night I didn't fall asleep without its babble the last sound I heard. My father worked the land for Major Hargreaves. My mother died when I was nine. That was when I first knew there were angels.

'I was in the parlour by mother's coffin. Oh, everything was so white and I was crying. I didn't want to live without her and father didn't seem to know what he was doing. Out of his mind with grief. And my mother so beautiful. I wanted to get in the coffin beside her.

'That was when I first saw the angels. There was no sound except the river and sunlight was pouring into the white room. Then the angel appeared by the side of the coffin.'

'What did it look like?'

'It was an angel, golden, with wings.'

She said it as you might speak of a saucepan to an idiot in the kitchen: 'It's big and round with a handle and a lid.'

'Have you always seen angels?'

'I always knew they were there, after that. But I saw them – actually saw them as I'm seeing you – only once more and that was when . . .'

Her speech trailed off and she fumbled with an ornament and looked away. Then she looked right at me.

'I was in love. He went off to the First War. A letter came. I was at his mother's house at the time. "Missing, believed killed."

'I had no need of that letter. I knew. That's why I'd gone round to his mother's. The previous night the angel appeared. Nothing was said . . . I mean, I didn't hear any words, but, as if spoken into my brain, "Charles has been killed, but it's all right."

'It wasn't all right, not for me. I loved him so. Never loved another.' And she laughed. She said, 'I knew I had to go to his Ma – he always called her Ma. So I went.'

'Did you tell her about the angel?'

'I told her I knew Charles was all right. Then I just found I was saying the Lord's Prayer and the Hail Mary out loud. I don't remember much else about that day.'

'What do you think these visions were? What are angels?'

'You should know that, Father. They're what we were always taught they are – messengers from God.'

This was the quality of Louie's faith: heavenly, spiritual things really were to her more substantial than things of the earth. If you had asked her what was the Holy Communion, she would have replied in an instant, 'The Body and Blood of Our Lord, of course' – as if you had asked a silly question.

Yet her faith was no caricature, no pantomime or parade of mythology. Her spiritual reality was solid. She simply had a radically different perspective from almost anyone else you could meet. It was not shallow but found always practical ways in which to reveal itself. A strict schoolmistress, Louie had been renowned for her acuteness and loved by even the most unwilling pupils. There were many of her former pupils in the parish. One said to me, 'She simply had a way with people – girls, staff, everyone. You felt better when she came into the room. You knew you couldn't say anything against her.'

I watched her dying. I was there on the very day. It was like watching someone being born. She made such a good job of it, such fun of it. That was one of her expressions: 'Dying will be fun!' Not that she was ever maudlin. There was no sentimentality about Louie, no 'half in love with easeful death'.

She had been taken back into hospital and put into a sideward with flowers and her own crucifix. The window looked out towards the drive and the gatehouse and Louie liked this situation: 'I want to be able to see people.'

On 29 June, St Peter's Day, I took her Holy Communion. She was having difficulty breathing but was as cheerful as ever. Taking the Sacrament seemed to tire her out and she lay back on her pillow. She was wheezing and snoring so that I thought she had fallen asleep.

Suddenly she gripped my hand and pulled herself up in bed. Her body seemed all lightness, as if she had stepped out of it. Her eyes moved from side to side as if she was watching the progress of something across the field of vision. She smiled and laughed and squeezed my hand more tightly. Her face – I could think only of the exultation at the 'Sanctus' in Mozart's 'C Minor Mass': two choirs hurling antiphonal heaven at each other across the vault: *Dominus, Deus, Sabbaoth. . .*

'You see, Father, they've come for me!'

She lay back slowly and died.

About a week later I was at the hospital to see someone else and I spent a few minutes talking to the night sister on Louie's ward.

'That woman,' said the sister, 'that woman! She was an angel!'

# 5

## Bomb warning

Armley, Leeds, is famous for its gaol but it has other attractions: a magnificent Victorian gothic parish church, a good library and a railway junction so wonderfully complex that it would rival the most baroque layout on a model track. Armley also had facilities which were attractive to Adolf Hitler in 1941: a munitions factory, two major road bridges and, of course, the railway goods yard itself and a gas works.

It was a densely populated area with congested rows of Victorian terraced houses bordering a piece of spare land known as 'the gaol field'. It was some sort of miracle that more of these houses, and the working people and their families within them, were not destroyed in Hitler's bombing raids. The Vicar of Armley at the time told me a story of one family's extraordinary escape.

The Arkwrights lived below the gaol, quite close to Castleton school and not far from another square of derelict land which everyone in Armley called 'the pit', though there had never been a local pit. Emily and John Arkwright had a daughter, Brenda, who attended the school. She was a bright, lively girl with ginger hair – 'a bit of a firecracker,' as the old Vicar told me.

Brenda was not a difficult child or naughty, but the sort who played hard and worked hard. In 1941, she was nine and in the next to top class at Castleton. But one day she was asked a question by the teacher and made no reply at all. 'She was sitting staring into space with her mouth wide open,' said Miss Cowie, the class teacher. She made a joke of it and called out, 'Close your mouth, Brenda, or you'll catch flies!'

The girl roused herself and answered the question at the second time of asking. Nothing would have been made of so small an incident except that it happened again and again until Miss Cowie asked Brenda to stay behind one playtime and tell her what was the trouble. At first she would say nothing and a few silent tears were shed.

'Come along, Brenda. This isn't at all like you. Tell me what's the matter and we'll see if we can put it right.'

The girl murmured only that nothing was the matter, but there were more tears. Miss Cowie did not press her, but reported the matter to the headteacher. Meanwhile, Brenda's behaviour gave more cause for anxiety. She ate little and started sleepwalking. Still no one could find out from her what was wrong.

In the end it was one of her close friends who went to see Miss Cowie and said, 'I know what's the matter with Brenda: she's seeing a lady who tells her things.'

Brenda overheard this and flew into a rage. When she had calmed down and they were alone, Miss Cowie said, 'Tell me all about it. Perhaps I've seen the lady myself.' She cuddled the little girl and gave her a barley sugar.

So the whole story came out. Brenda had first seen the lady standing by the school gate. Then she had started to appear suddenly, during lessons or at home in Brenda's own room.

'What is she like?'

'She's like Jesus' mother in the picture Bible.'

'Are you afraid?'

'No.'

'What does she say to you?'

It turned out that, at first, the apparition had said nothing, but then she had begun to tell Brenda that she and her parents must get out of their house or else something dreadful would happen to them. Brenda had told her parents but they accused her of 'romancing', making it all up. When at last they met Miss Cowie and discussed the whole affair, Emily Arkwright said, 'You know what an over-active imagination that girl has got.'

It was true. Brenda *was* very imaginative. Her stories were the best of all the class and her pictures the wildest. But when faced by her mother and father and Miss Cowie all together,

Brenda flew into a tantrum and said they were ganging up on her and she *was* telling the truth. The adults talked quietly to her but they were at a loss for what to do.

One morning Brenda did not get up for school when she was called. Her mother was angry because she herself had to get to work and she had not time on her hands to be running after lazy children. But when she went into Brenda's bedroom she was terrified. The child was lying rigid, ashen, unconscious. When her mother could not waken her, she thought she was dead.

They had no telephone but a neighbour a few doors away had let it be known that his could always be used in an emergency. Emily Arkwright phoned Dr Platt, who came at once. Meanwhile John had managed to rouse Brenda a little and, though she was still lying down, she had her eyes open. Dr Platt examined the child and then asked the parents to leave him alone with her for a few minutes.

He emerged to tell them that there was nothing wrong with their daughter that could not easily be put right. She was getting up and it would be a good idea for her to be given some tea and toast.

'He told them,' said the Vicar, 'that he would ask me to call. I remember it clearly. He drove up to my door in a fearful hurry and blurted out straightaway that he had a patient who was seeing visions. He said he thought there was nothing seriously the matter. The child was highly strung, rather hysterical. But he didn't have the time to spend listening to her – he had a flu epidemic on his hands.

'So I went round. Brenda and her folks were sitting at the kitchen table. She looked weak and fearful. They were watching her and obviously they were worried to death. They weren't regular churchgoers but I had seen them at Christmas and Easter and I had baptized Brenda.

'I said I would like to be left alone with her and I asked Brenda about her visions. I told her that other little girls had seen visions, so she was not that unusual. This seemed to cheer her up a bit. I remember, she asked me if I had ever seen a vision and I was bound to answer that I had not.

'She did not actually say that the vision was the Virgin Mary, only that she looked like her. I asked her what the vision said and she replied that the lady didn't say anything "with her mouth" but that she could still hear her voice "in my head".

'Then she was very upset and started to shake all over. She cried a little and said that the lady had told her their house was going to be bombed and they must leave it and stay somewhere else. I asked her if she knew when this was supposed to happen and she said, "Tonight."

'She was distraught. "Tell them! Tell them! *You* tell them – they'll *believe* you!" She was shouting and crying, making so much noise that her parents came back in. Brenda ran and buried her head in her mother's pinafore. She took her out and I was left with John.

'I said, "You know what the girl has been saying – well, the reason she's so upset today is that she's convinced it's going to happen tonight. She's quite certain and you won't budge her. Is there anywhere you can go just for the night? And then tomorrow you'll be able to come back and reassure her."

'He asked me outright if I thought there was anything in "this visions business".

'I said what I thought: that young girls like Brenda were famous for "seeing things" and that she had no doubt often looked at a picture of the Virgin Mary and it was haunting her vivid imagination. But it had been going on for a while. . .

' "So you think," he said, "there might be something in it?"

'I said something rather untheological – that there was no harm in playing safe, just for one night anyway.

'They made an arrangement with John's sister in Upper Wortley, a couple of miles away. "Anything for a quiet life," as Emily said.

'That night a bomb fell on their house and it was destroyed. There were three or four more blitzed at about the same time. The authorities cleared up the mess and children use the gaps in the terraces as shortcuts on the way to school nowadays.

'I visited the family twice at John's sister's. I took Brenda a rosary which one of the congregation had brought back from Lourdes. She learned of Brenda's story and thought she ought to have it. Brenda didn't become extra devout or start coming to church regularly. She became her old rumbustious self. As far as I know, she did not see the lady again.'

# 6
....
# *All in the mind?*

The characteristic appearance of ghosts is not such that the person who sees one invariably comes away and says, 'Oh yes, that was definitely a ghost!' Part of the eeriness is created by the very element of doubt: was it really a ghost or only a trick of the light – or even trick of the digestion?' As Scrooge at first said to the shade of Jacob Marley, 'There's more gravy than grave about you. Why, you could be an undigested piece of cheese!' The powerful flavour of all ghostly experiences is atmosphere.

I was once Vicar of a parish in Civil War country and our church still carried the scars of that conflict. The heavy oak door, for example, fitted in 1633 and always referred to as 'the new door', bore the marks of the Roundhead soldiers' vandalism. At the Battle of Marston Moor, 1644, they had held Royalist prisoners in the church and carved caricatures of King Charles with their bayonets on the door. Time hallows even our loutishness, however, and these eyesores have become minor treasures in their way. The parish guide always points them out to American tourists!

The church traces its origins back to Saxon times: there are stone crosses from that era, restored and turned upright, in the churchyard. On a ledge in the nave is preserved (or half preserved) a fourteenth-century stone skull which was discovered, intact and grinning, also in the churchyard, in 1935, but which someone dropped and broke in two in 1936.

There is also a Jacobean lectern which, incredibly, a nineteenth-century sidesman and stoker of the church boiler used as a chopping-block! There is a gash in this poor varnished bird's neck, otherwise she has been perfectly restored to her original position and purpose and now stands vigilant under the hymnboard, looking as if she will peck any member of the congregation who dares to fall asleep during the sermon.

Tales of the supernatural are routine in such a place. Once a lady putting the finishing touches to her display for a flower festival caught sight of what she took to be a pile of old clothes in the south-west corner. It was dusk and she was alone in the building. She made a note to remove the clothes on her way out. 'But,' she said, 'I suddenly saw the "pile of clothes" stand up and walk across the back of the church from one side to the other and disappear through the wall. It looked like a soldier and he seemed to be wounded. I never finished that pedestal of flowers!'

Then there was Ray Morton, a churchwarden who always stayed behind after the morning service to put the kneelers straight and tidy the hymnbooks. As he reached the back pew one day he became vaguely aware of a figure standing by the lectern as if searching the Bible for a particular lesson.

He began a casual conversation with the figure in the unselfconscious way people often do when they are working at some light routine.

'I wondered why I was getting no answer. I thought maybe he was engrossed in looking for his passage in the book. Then, when I'd stacked all the books, I stood up straight and stared right at him. It was a monk – cowl over his head and everything! He never made a sound. He walked two or three paces into the middle of the choir and vanished!'

This was Ray's favourite story and he would trot it out at every parish gathering, telling the tale in his deep, resonant voice. It was his tone that made the choirboys shudder with excitement and terror – and just an ounce of scepticism. I would accuse him of having been at the homebrew, but he only said, 'Not likely, Vicar, it was only half past eleven in the morning!'

One of the choirboys, David Fish, met me one morning in the vestry and asked, 'D'you think there are such things as ghosts, Vicar?'

It was a warm summer morning and the church was filled with sunlight, so the thought of ghosts was academic rather than oppressive.

'I don't know, David. People say they've seen all sorts of strange things. What do *you* think?'

He was adamant: 'I'm sure there are ghosts. And I'm sure they come to give us a message.'

'Like angels, you mean? That's what "angel" means, you know – "a messenger".'

He went red, as if angels were rather childish things for big boys to talk about. 'I'm not sure I believe in angels, Vicar.'

'What kind of a thing is that to say? You're so certain of ghosts but you're doubtful when it comes to angels. What's the difference?'

There was a picture of huge, winged Gabriel on the vestry wall. It was the Annunciation. The angel looked stern. Moreover, he seemed not to be looking at Mary but out of the picture and into the room. It was one of those pictures where the eyes seem to follow you as you move about – 'guilty conscience pictures' I have heard them called. David gave the picture a nervous glance. He said, 'There are ghosts in the Bible, though, aren't there?'

'A few. But far more angels.'

He became all conspiratorial: 'Sometimes when I'm in church by myself, putting out the hymn lists, I feel as if there's someone watching me. Once there was an old lady sitting at the back. She never made a sound. I hadn't seen her before – ever. I was sure she was a ghost. She just sat there and stared straight ahead. I was scared stiff. Then the church began to fill up. It's a funny thing – I kept looking down into the nave for that old lady all through the service, but I never saw her again. She just vanished!'

'Vanished? Old ladies are often *little* old ladies. She'd have got hidden behind a big fella like Mr Dale or Mr Hetherington. Old ladies don't vanish!'

'But there's more to it than that, Vicar. You know how stuff gets left behind after a service?'

'Two umbrellas and a pair of gloves last week alone.'

'Well, when I went out of church that same morning, I noticed a white handkerchief in the pew just where the old lady had been sitting. When I first saw her she was holding a white hanky.'

'That proves it then! She was real enough. Or do *your* ghosts blow their noses? I'm sure angels don't have to!'

He looked unconvinced. I looked back at stern Gabriel.

David continued, 'It was the atmosphere, though. You know, when I looked at the old lady she just seemed so unreal, weird. It wasn't like looking at a real person.'

At once there was a loud rattling. The latch on the vestry door jerked up and down and two of David's friends rushed in. David and I noticed the startled look in each other's eyes and we both laughed. That sudden rattling had done more than enough to make me sceptical of my scepticism. Atmosphere. . .

The Friday after my conversation with David there was a parish trip to York Minster to hear Bruckner's 'Te Deum' and Mozart's 'Coronation Mass' – music in glass and stone, the best sound this side of heaven. The performance finished at about half past nine and we set off home by coach. It was warm, sultry summertime, the sun low in the sky over the flat land; the trees motionless.

Two parishioners got off at their cottage between the villages and I moved up and sat in their seat at the front of the bus. The driver was new to Lister's Coaches, new to the area in fact, and I wanted to make sure he knew about the short cut over Marston Moor. He said, 'Yes thanks. I've had my instructions from Jack.'

Just as he finished speaking, I looked ahead out of the panoramic window. Not far in front, by the roadside, stood a cavalier. He was in full uniform and wore a real sword. The shock made me shiver as if the blade of that sword were being stroked up and down my spine. I couldn't speak. The driver seemed not to notice the apparition. It never moved, simply smiled up at the coach as we passed.

In a minute we were disembarking by the lychgate. I almost felt I should seek out David Fish at once and tell him what I had seen, but he had been sitting at the back of the coach singing not quite respectable songs with the other choirboys on the way home. As they jumped off the bus, they were still involved in their camaraderie and games. I put off the idea of talking to him until Sunday morning.

I went back inside the coach to where the driver was bending among the seats to make sure no one had left anything behind.

'Look,' I said, 'you'll probably think I've gone barmy, but did you see anything on the road back there?'

'See anything?' he asked in that mildly incredulous style which people adopt when they have been asked a stupid question. 'Nothing – except the bloke in the uniform.' He spoke as if the vision had been perfectly natural, as if the ancient soldier had been a present day tommy from the local army camp and his flamboyant uniform had been khaki.

'So you did see him them?'

'Well, you couldn't miss him, dressed like that, could you?'

He went on shutting the bus windows with a matter-of-factness which was definitely this-worldly. I didn't know whether I should feel more or less unnerved. Which was worse – to be unbalanced enough to have hallucinations or to be unfortunate enough to see ghosts?

'Sealed Knot,' said the driver.

I thought he was talking about securing the windows and simply stood with my mouth open.

'Sealed Knot,' he repeated. 'The society that gets together and replays all the old battles. Well, it's Marston Moor week, isn't it?'

I had had no idea. It was my first year in the parish. And it was indeed Marston Moor week – the first week in July, when the Sealed Knot society always comes to re-enact the 1644 battle. The figure I had seen on the road had no doubt been one of the advance party come to reconnoitre the country in time for the mock struggle which was to take place the following day. And my fright had been caused by nothing more terrifying than a solicitor or accountant from York practising for his costumed hobby.

Perhaps. For I spoke some years later with an old parishioner who remembered once stopping his car on Marston Moor in a storm to pick up a member of the Sealed Knot (as he thought) who was getting a real drenching. But when, having bent to open the passenger-door, he looked up – there was no one to be seen.

# 7

....

# *Whistler*

The Reverend Walter Taylor was Vicar of one of the country parishes in the rural deanery. There were eight parishes and Walter's was the most remote and the most beautiful – in limestone country where the River Wharfe begins its babbling journey through the Yorkshire Dales.

Walter knew every bend in that river, every tree on the pastel green fell, every stile, gate, farm, outbuilding and pond in the 60 square miles of his parish. After all, he had been Vicar of Ramston for 40 years. I occasionally went walking with him and his dogs and he would say, 'Yes, I think they accepted me in the village after the first 30 years. Any road, that's when they realized they were stuck with me! Getting used to folk – what the BBC calls "relationships" – takes longer in the country, you know.'

They all knew him, they said, by his whistle: whistling for his dogs, whistling over a good hand of dominoes on Friday night in the Acorn pub – or just whistling an unidentifiable tune. He was nicknamed 'Whistler'.

He was a painter, too. Of landscapes. *The* landscape of his dale and fell, which itself resembled a completed watercolour. Walter looked as if he was part of that landscape, as if he had always been there. In fact, though, he was not a countryman. He had been born and brought up in Sheffield. He would say, 'I'm a countryman by adoption and grace.' He had learned to love his adoptive element and was fond of quoting the poet William Cowper: 'God made the country and man made the town.'

Ramston teemed with tourists from March to November and to visitors it was picturesque. But, like all the upper Dales villages, it was more than a pretty picture; it was a place of work and struggle. 'Some of those folk who race through in their motor cars and stop by the bridge to take photographs should try their hand at rescuing a sheep stuck in a ditch,' Walter would comment. 'I never understood the parable of the Lost Sheep properly until I came out here in '36!'

Walter knew his parish because he had shared in its work and had walked every inch of it time and again. He used to say, 'You don't know a tune until you can whistle it and you don't know your land until you've walked it.' He once told me, 'You start to know the folk in a place when you've christened them – and when you've christened their children as well.' He had even married some of the children of those he had christened before the war.

No one could say that Walter was not of the earth, earthy, but he had an unearthly interest; he was an expert on the subject of Dales ghosts. I even tried to put all his stories together in a book once, but Walter always preferred the spoken word over anything written down. And he could talk! I have been on an eight-mile walk with him, up one side of the dale and back down the other, and heard him tell one story after another all day, and even at the end he had not run out of material. He was a wonderful raconteur who could hold after-dinner audiences spellbound. No wonder he preferred the spoken word over 'writing things down'!

He would tell the tale, for instance, of a church where children who had died in an epidemic in the nineteenth century were buried in lead coffins in the crypt. 'There have been many occasions when people have heard singing from the crypt, a choir, children's songs. Ghosthunters from London came to investigate that case.'

Then he would swing his stick and whistle for the dogs, giving you time for the story to sink in. He was adept at creating atmosphere, was Walter, and had a consummate sense of timing. He could become a scary figure when he stopped still on a rise above the bend in the river at sunset and recounted a ghost story in a penetrative whisper, pointing his stick in the direction of the weird occurrence at the same time.

'The cottage on yon hill is haunted – the one with the white front. A sheep man lived there all his life and the story has it that folk used to see him walking the fells as usual long after he'd died. Not weird at all, they said. Almost matter of fact – until you remembered that the chap who'd just walked past you had been dead for 15 years.

'The Vicarage looks across the river to the white cottage. It must be about a mile and a half away. No one lives in it now, but I've seen lights come on across there late at night.'

I said Walter had been Vicar of Ramston for 40 years, but that is not quite true. He had been Vicar for more than 39 years. He was ordained in 1926 and went to Ramston ten years later, after a curacy in Barnsley and a spell as a vicar in Rochdale. So the fortieth anniversary of his coming to Ramston coincided with his Golden Jubilee as a priest. There was to be a double celebration in the parish church. Walter himself had planned the service and was to preach a thanksgiving sermon. His parishioners were arranging a reception in the village hall at which only locals would be present. Ramston was not the sort of parish which took much interest in the centralized authority of the Bradford diocese. As Walter once told me, 'We nearly declared UDI t'other year!' His Jubilee had been mentioned in the announcements column of the *Church Times*, however, and so it was thought that one or two people who had known Walter in his Barnsley or Rochdale days might also turn up.

But three days before the celebrations, Walter died. Mrs Crawford who 'did' for him – he had never married – explained: 'He'd just come in off the fell with the dogs as usual. It was nearly lunchtime but I called to him and asked if he'd like a cup of tea. He called back, "Thanks. Just let me get my boots off," and he toddled off across the yard, whistling as usual. That was the last I heard of him, poor Walter. I took the tea in and he was sitting in his chair, the morning paper across his knee. I was talking away, chattering like you do, and I thought it was funny when I got no reply. Of course when I got close I knew straightaway.

'Poor old soul. But I'd never have believed it. Ask anyone

and they'd say old Walter would have made a century and got the Queen's telegram. But you never know when it's your turn, do you?'

The parishioners decided to go ahead with the arrangements, only now Walter's Jubilee was to be his memorial service. He was 77. The memorial service was to be held in the evening after the funeral in the afternoon. An Assistant Bishop in the diocese would come and preach. There were kindly jokes about how Walter would miss all the food and drink got in specially!

The service was held on Michaelmas Day. It had rained for 24 hours and then stopped in the early evening and a mist had fallen. Autumn mists and fogs can be extremely dense in the Yorkshire Dales, even so early in the year, and especially after heavy rain. On that day the wind dropped and it was as if the whole dale had been soundproofed. At seven o'clock there was a muffled clatter as the village folk made their way to the church, which stood apart, like a lonely ship on the ocean. Robust voices and favourite hymns soon rose from it: 'O Thou Who Camest from Above' and 'Praise the Lord, Ye Heavens Adore Him!' The Bishop surprised everyone by turning out to have known Walter better than anyone had suspected. There were even one or two restrained jokes and the usual sort of respectful chuckles.

Later, across at the hall, it was a more rumbustious affair, for, as many said, 'Walter wouldn't have wanted anybody to be sad.' I knew most of the locals there by sight, if not by name, and a handful of folk had turned up from Walter's previous incarnations in Barnsley and Lancashire. I met a bald, red-faced, middle-aged clergyman over a vol-au-vent. He wore a tweed jacket and an amazingly broad dog collar. He was plump and hearty, and came from Lincoln. It turned out that Walter had been his Vicar in Rochdale and had prepared him for Confirmation.

'It was Walter who first put into my head the idea that I might be a priest. I was 14 at the time. I haven't seen Walter for . . . it must 42 years. I knew he was up in Yorkshire somewhere and then I saw his notice in the *Church Times*. It was only when I phoned to check the time of the service that I heard he'd gone to his reward.

'I had a hard time getting here as well. The mist came down like a curtain – and then when it got dark! I don't know these "B" roads, but luckily I saw someone walking so I stopped. He said he was going to Ramston and he would ride with me, if I didn't mind letting his dogs in the back of the car.

'So I'd no more trouble after that. I dropped him outside the Vicarage and he strode off with his dogs. I heard him whistling long after he was out of sight.'

# 8

## *The suburban devil*

I was once a curate in the parish of Manston, a suburb of Leeds. It was, still is, a neat, quiet, out of town parish, a mixture of private houses and council dwellings. One of the more agreeable pastoral jobs was to go and sit in the parish room – a part of the Vicarage in which the Vicar didn't live – and be on duty for marriage interviews. Often no one came, so you could have a couple of hours at your book. Couples came to put in their banns and to ask which hymns they could have – usually 205 and 311 in *Hymns Ancient & Modern* (revised), but a favourite was the 1960s pop dirge 'A Whiter Shade of Pale', which made the Vicar turn a paler shade of death when they asked for it; and, once, 'A Groovy Kind of Love', which was not as kinky as it might appear, being based on a piano sonata by Clementi. Mostly they came to book the wedding a year in advance because the hotels required that much notice to reserve the reception.

I was sitting in the parish room one Friday evening in 1971 and was getting ready to shut up shop as it was almost nine o'clock. It had been a warm May day and I had sat with the door wide open, looking out at the pink and white blossom. I must have turned my back for a moment. When I turned to face the door, I saw a startlingly elegant woman of about 50 with long yellow hair, wearing a white dress. She looked like a real life piece of mythology.

'Can I speak?' She could barely talk for emotion.

I gave her a chair and she sat still and silent for a long time. Then she said, 'It's my son. He's possessed by the Devil.'

Certainly this was a change from, 'We've booked the Manston for three o'clock on July 16th, so can we get married at half past one please?'

I think I mumbled something like, 'What d'you mean,

"possessed"?' Then I thought how foolish it was for a parson to say such a thing. I realized I had been like a little boy sitting by the riverbank all those hours catching only minnows, but who now had a pike on the line and was about to make a mess of landing it. I began again: 'I'll come at once.'

'No. It's no good. He's not at home. That's the only reason I've been able to come out. If he knew I was here he'd kill me.'

She wore a light, blossomy perfume. Her arms were bare and she clasped them in front of herself. I asked if she were cold. She said, 'No, no. It's him! He makes me like this. I'm not usually nervous. I'm not neurotic or anything, whatever you may think.'

She calmed down and began to speak slowly and deliberately, as if reciting a speech she had practised to perfection: 'He comes in and goes to his room. He's 19. He lights candles and sets them up in front of the mirror. I know it's a thing he learned in Borstal. He has bits of animals – it's too disgusting. He does things to his face. And he shouts and throws himself about. The door's locked and he won't let me in. Some of the noises he makes you wouldn't believe. He cuts himself. There's always a foul smell. Can you do anything, please? I'm sure he'll kill himself before long.'

This was no minnow. I cast around for something to say. 'Has he had any treatment from a psychiatrist?'

She coughed and gave me a disgusted look. 'In prison, yes. But it's not a doctor he needs. He needs a priest. He needs an exorcism.'

'When d'you expect him back?'

'Tomorrow, day after tomorrow. Next week maybe. I don't know.'

'Let's go across to church.'

'No!' She seemed alarmed. 'No, I don't want to go into the church.'

'Where do you live?'

'Off Crossgates Lane.'

'Let me walk home with you, then?'

'Not now, no. Can you come tomorrow? Come early

tomorrow.' She was pacing, her high heels clattering on the bare boards.

'Won't you sit down and I'll say a prayer?'

She stood still, her eyes wary while I said the Our Father. I took her name and address. I made sure she had my telephone number.

'You will come tomorrow, in the morning?'

I promised I would. She walked out of the door and down the path as unexceptionally as any girl come to put in the banns.

On Fridays the Vicar was in Middlesbrough at the Lodge, so I spoke to him after Matins the following day. He said, 'You never know. It's most likely a cock and bull story. But you'd better get the exorcist in just in case. Come across to the Vicarage and I'll give you his number.'

I had had a bad night and that expression, 'cock and bull', put yet more black magic pictures of the cinematographic kind into my head.

At the Vicarage, the Vicar's wife was in the kitchen. She asked me if I would like some cheese on toast, but the Vicar carried on as if the question had never been put: 'Come into the study, Peter.'

He took a dog-eared book out of his desk drawer. 'There, that's the fella you want.'

So there really was an exorcist – the 'diocesan exorcist', he was called. Times change – now there was only one exorcist for the whole diocese, whereas in the second century Tertullian had said that any Christian priest who could not exorcise demons should be put to death.

I rang the gentleman as soon as I got home and he arrived just before nine o'clock. He was a swarthy miniature with a black moustache which he seemed to wear like a disguise. My eyes were immediately drawn to his huge suitcase. He would not have a cup of tea, he said in his ethereal voice. So we set off at once. He walked very briskly, smoking one cigarette after the other.

'What's the form? I mean, what will you do when we arrive?'

'I want to hear what your Wilkie Collins heroine says first.'

The Wilkie Collins heroine was now dressed in jeans and a sweatshirt. As soon as we were inside the house, the exorcist made the sign of the Cross and invoked the name of the Holy Trinity in Latin. Now he would have a cup of tea, please. He sat next to the woman on the sofa and held her hand as she told him what she had already told me.

The house stank of dust and rotting vegetables. Dirty pots and pans were piled up in the sink and there was a monotonous dripping from an overhead pipe. The exorcist said he would like to see the boy's room. There was only a bare bulb over the upstairs landing. The bathroom door was open, but the boy's door, at the end of the passage, was locked. The woman had a key.

As she had said the night before, it was disgusting. It smelt of dead flesh, stale flesh and cannabis. Two half-burned candles were set in front of a mirror on the dressing-table. There was a dirty pen-knife and a pornographic magazine. The boy's clothes were scattered all about the place. His bed was unmade.

The exorcist again made the sign of the Cross, calling out in a loud voice, 'In the name of the Father and of the Son and of the Holy Ghost. Amen.'

He opened his case. I was surprised to see that it really did contain bell, book and candle. There was also a beautiful blue rosary, a bulky, rather savage crucifix and a phial of holy water. He got me to hold the crucifix aloft as he walked about, sprinkling the walls with the water and commanding any evil spirits to return, in the name of Christ, to their own place.

Downstairs the door slammed. I looked at the woman. We were both thinking the same thought. But it turned out to be the postman delivering a parcel from a mail order company. The exorcist repeated the Our Father and the Gloria and we went downstairs.

I marvelled at his capacity for tea in that atmosphere. While drinking another cup, he noted the boy's age, name and which Borstal he had been in. He enquired about the woman's husband and she told him he was dead. Then he took a card from his pocket and said, 'You have Father Peter's phone number. Here's mine.'

'Oh, thank you, Father. Thank you both.' Her expression was still one of terror, but her voice was all relief. The exorcist had gone about his business in such a matter-of-fact style that he might have been a salesman, his suitcase full of brushes. He smiled a lot and that helped. He had that aura of dapper unflappability about him which is legendarily associated with World War II fighter pilots.

As we walked back through the shopping centre, I asked him, 'What did you think, then – is the place possessed?'

'It's hard to say. There's not always a clear line to be drawn. If you ask me, I'd say he's been messing about, experimenting with snippets of nastiness he's learned in the Borstal – or else read in the Sunday papers. His mother's a problem, though, as you saw. You will keep an eye on her, won't you?'

'Do you really believe there are demons?'

He gave me the sort of look the salesman would have given me if I had asked him whether he believed in brushes.

'Oh yes. It's pretty rare though – the real thing. There's a huge grey area involving kinky sex, people looking for a thrill, neurotics, mental illness. But yes, now and again, the real thing.'

'What's it like – the real thing?'

'Very, very frightening. Distressing and depressing. It's like looking at nothing, emptiness. How can I explain? It's as if you're looking at evil and there isn't any good anywhere at all. You know, evil only exists as a parody of goodness. I mean, there can be lies only where the concept of truth is valued. We recognize hatred because we see it as the opposite of love, and so on. But when you see radical evil – demonic possession if you like – it's as if there's only evil, that's what makes it terrifying, not some carnival Devil, vampire, toad or whatever.

'It removes the apprehension of all goodness and of God himself. It makes you cringe and vomit. "Weeping and gnashing of teeth", as it says in the Bible.'

'Why do you get involved with it, do this job?'

'I don't rightly know.'

'D'you think you're chosen for it?'

He stopped and faced me by the telephone kiosk. 'Not chosen, Peter, singled out.'

He called back at my home and I phoned a taxi to return him to his own place. He told me that most of the black magic stories you read about in the newspapers are connected with a bored, rich lunatic fringe who live in the more affluent suburbs and secluded villages. 'It's all money, power and perverted sex. Devilish enough, but not in the supposed sense of the world. There's a lot of blackmail and violence. They like to scare you. It's the wide range of their connections that scares me. You never know where one of them will pop up next. They're in all the professions – including ours. And they get whatever they like printed in the papers.'

I received startling confirmation of all this. On the following Monday, the headline in the evening paper ran 'EXORCISM IN CROSSGATES' over a picture of the diocesan exorcist. The brief story underneath was inaccurate and vague. But there could be no doubting the fact that those who were concerned with such matters wanted to leave him in no uncertainty about their knowledge of his whereabouts.

The woman in white left the parish not long after that. I think she remarried and went to live in Wiltshire. Anyhow, I was relieved to be rid of the matter and since that time I have kept as far away from these issues as possible. Cowardly, perhaps. But I did not feel 'singled out' and I had sensed something horribly close to the emptiness of which the exorcist had spoken. It is terrifyingly true: there is weeping and gnashing of teeth.

# 9
....
## *Out of body*

While I was at theological college in the English countryside, I became acquainted with a man training for the priesthood who 'dabbled' in spiritual experience of a dubious sort. The consequences were terrifying and, for the man concerned, extremely destructive.

It began with a dream. Stephen recounted this dream to a group of us over coffee after Compline. Or was it a dream? It was in fact an out-of-body experience long before these experiences became widely reported and theorized about.

'I was in bed,' said Stephen, 'and dreaming. I seemed to rise out of bed and drift towards the ceiling.' This provoked some laughter because Stephen was by far the meatiest chap in college. He went on: 'I could see myself asleep in bed. It struck me as funny and intriguing. So I watched. It really was me. I watched as I turned over in my sleep, noticing an arm come out from under the covers and withdraw again out of the cold.

'I don't know how long it continued but it felt like an hour, perhaps longer. Then I seemed to hear a voice – well, it was in my head – say that it was time for me to go back down. I didn't want to go back. I don't know why, but I felt a terrific sadness. It was pleasant being out of my body and I felt free. I felt I could see things more clearly, that I could think more clearly; that I had a true perspective. The ordinary bodily existence seemed a dull thing beside this.

'When I woke up in bed I felt really sad. It was like a depression, a weight on me, and I went around with it for days. Daily life seemed empty somehow and I craved for what I regarded as the purer, more spiritual state – which also seemed to be a state of greater awareness, a better state of being.

'After a few weeks it happened again. It was like returning home. Only this time it was even better. I didn't stay in my bedroom but floated out along the corridors – all around the college, except in the chapel. For some reason I felt uneasy about going into the chapel.

'I went outside on to the lawn, which was dewy and moonlit. I thought, "It would nice to go up to the summer-house." The next I knew, there I was beside the summer-house, smelling the blossom on the night air. It was so lovely I could have wept for sheer joy.'

Stephen said that on waking this time he had an even greater sense of loss than before. The out-of-body world had become more real to him than the world of waking experience.

This changed order of priorities brought about a change in his behaviour, which I witnessed directly. He became irritable and impatient. In a lecture on Christian doctrine he scorned the tutor and claimed in as many words that such study of doctrine was for 'groundlings'. *He*, by contrast, enjoyed immediate, unblinkered spiritual experience!

As time went by, this sense of being superior to other members of the college intensified. Stephen's attitude can be best described as, 'Don't bother me, I've got better things to do than to talk to you!'

The staff knew what was going on – not least because Stephen never made any secret of it. But they were wise. They concluded that he was going through a passing phase or some sort of obsession. Like Mr Toad with his motor car, Stephen was in the grip of a new craze. The staff believed he would grow out of it.

Meanwhile, Stephen became more and more of a spiritual bore. People took off in the opposite direction when they saw him coming. He was no longer invited to post-Compline coffee parties. It was difficult to ignore his self-righteous sniffs and snorts in the doctrine lectures and to live within 100 yards of his overbearing attitude to everything and anyone.

What drew his next-door neighbour to his room one night was his screams. He was calling out – 'gurgling', as one of those who went to his aid put it – for someone to come and save him, to bring him back. There was a commotion such that half of the college was wakened by it.

I heard the details the next day while Stephen was under sedation. Mike, Stephen's neighbour and the best thing he had left to a friend, was first on the scene. He told me that he found Stephen lying rigid on top of his bedclothes, white-faced, wild-eyed and screaming the place down. Other men arrived on the scene and Stephen began to flail about so that they had to restrain him. Mike said that it took the best part of half an hour to calm him down. When he was quieter, the others left and Mike remained while Stephen told quite a different story about his spiritual experiences from those we had all heard before.

He had learned, he said, how to go into the out-of-body experience almost at will. Moreover, he was able to direct his experience to visit such places as he desired. The 'trips' were always pleasant and the sensation which they generated bordered on the euphoric. He was, as he said, always sad to have to wake up. And over this part of the experience – just when to wake up – he had developed no control.

On this occasion he had willed his out-of-body self to go into the garden, but his reverie there had turned to horror. At first it was as before: fragrant, peaceful and hospitable. But, turning behind a row of bushes by the summer-house, he had been suddenly confronted with an altogether different land-scape, or dreamscape. He was on the edge of a cemetery and bodies were rising out of the graves. There was a cacophony as accompaniment: 'hellish-like spoilt music', as he said. There were snakes and unbelievably horrible creatures of nightmare staring at him and devouring one another. 'And,' he told Mike, 'there was the stench of putrefaction,' which he could not get out of his nostrils.

He tried to run, only to find he could not move. He thought he would die. Then he was able to move and his one thought was to reach the college chapel, for he believed he would be safe there. But when he scrambled, pursued by the nightmare apparitions, as far as the door of the chapel, he found it locked. (As a matter of fact, in ordinary everyday life, the chapel was never locked.)

It was then that he felt he was running out of breath and that he would die from lack of air. At that moment some men approached him from side doors of the house and began to drag him to safety. But he only tried to fight them off, calling out that he must get into the chapel, for only there would he be truly safe. This was obviously the time when the men had been struggling with him in his own room.

In a sense, Stephen recovered. I could say that he became as penitent as old Scrooge after his visitation by the three ghosts. He made a point of seeing each member of the college and apologizing for his bumptious behaviour. He buckled down to his studies with perseverance and humility. The staff were even more convinced that his conduct had indeed been only a phase and that he was no worse for it – even that it had been some sort of lesson to him.

But Stephen himself did not take that view. He announced that at the end of the year he would leave the college and give up his vocation. He actually completed that year's course and performed well in the examinations. The staff were quite willing for him to proceed, but he had made up his mind.

I went for a walk with him during the last week of term. It was a drowsy summer day, all bright colours and birdsong. I suppose I said what many others had said: 'Forget it, Steve. Put it down to experience. Concentrate on preparing yourself for ordination.'

He smiled and paused in his lumbering walk. 'I can't, you know. I just know I can't. That particular door is closed to me.'

So Stephen's experience became a living sermon to us, a demonstration of the truth that supernatural experiences alone are no mark or qualification of spiritual progress. The person who sees visions or dreams is not necessarily more holy than the great majority who do not. 'Try the spirits, whether they are of God.'

# 10

## *Things to come*

How do we know the difference between a supernatural experience and a *heightened* natural experience? It is possible that some strange occurrences are quite natural, though not explicable in terms of our present scientific understanding. Maybe things which seem remarkable now – like devastatingly accurate examples of precognition or clairvoyance – will come to be regarded as commonplace in future centuries. Some think that our present experience of our own psychic powers may be a dawning awareness of their existence – and these powers will become stronger and more usual in our species as we evolve.

Most people have had some experience of psychic awareness, a kind of knowledge which does not come to us through the senses. For instance, you are sitting there and you 'know' that the phone will ring – and it does. You sit down to write a letter to someone you have not heard from for years: suddenly a letter from that person falls onto the mat.

People also have premonitions of life's big events such as important meetings and journeys or even of approaching death. Perhaps the phenomenon of 'love at first sight' is really an example of precognition somehow, or at any rate something related to it: you see someone for the first time in your life and yet you feel you have known them for centuries. Perhaps you have!

..........

I have had two experiences of detailed premonition – sometimes called *déjà vu* – in my life: one happened when I was a boy of seven and the other when I had been ordained for about 15 years. Both occasions involved the act of moving house.

The first time was when my uncle and aunt had decided to leave the Leeds suburb where they had lived for many years to settle in the country. Having chosen a house in a village between York and Malton, they took my mother and father and me to see it. My uncle had a car, a Riley, of which he was very proud. Not many 'ordinary' people owned cars in those days just after the Second World War and my parents certainly did not. So it was always a treat when Uncle Alan offered to take us out 'for a run'.

I had, of course, never been to the village where they were going to live. I had been past it, but 15 miles to the south of it, on a trip from Leeds to Scarborough. But in those days, a lad growing up in a family without a car would have been unusual indeed if he had seen more than his own town, a few neighbouring beauty spots and the main roads leading to popular seaside resorts such as Scarborough and Blackpool. That is how it was with me exactly.

It was a lovely summer day and Aunt Edith had packed a picnic. We were all laughing and chattering in the car and we played a game that I like – the one where you count the 'legs' on the pubs you pass and score two for, as it might be, the Green Man, four for the Dog and Gun, and so on.

Unfortunately, when we were right out in the country, the car suffered a puncture. 'Unfortunately', I say, but it was fun for me to watch my uncle and my father jack up the old Riley and fix the wheel, and it also meant we began the picnic early. As we were sitting on car rugs in the corner of a field, Uncle Alan said, 'We're only a couple of miles off the village where we're going to live.'

I remember with absolute technicolour clarity the next few minutes. As he said the word 'village', I immediately 'saw' a road with a long bend in it, a church with a tower covered in ivy and a pub called the Crown. I also saw a postbox and a telephone and a telephone kiosk. I even remember thinking, 'What a pity – we score no "legs" for the Crown!'

We gathered our crockery and rolled up the car rugs, and in a few minutes we rounded a long bend and Uncle Alan said,

'We're here, folks!' And there was the church and the pub, the telephone kiosk and the postbox. I was very troubled by it. This must have been noticeable because on the way home Aunt Edith said, 'You're quiet, Peter!'

When I was alone with my father, I told him about it. He said, 'Don't let it worry you, son. These things happen sometimes. You have to think of it as a True Dream.'

I said, 'But it wasn't a dream! I wasn't even asleep!'

'Then you'll have to think of it as a little bit of magic, won't you? But don't tell your Auntie Edith: she's very superstitious.' (That was how and when I learned the meaning of 'superstition'.)

..........

My second experience of precognition was a dream. At the time I was chaplain and head of RE at a school in Bolton, and I received a letter from the Archbishop of York inviting me to consider a move to be vicar of a rural parish in Yorkshire. Partly because I was born in Yorkshire and also because I had served some time in my teaching post, I was attracted by the offer. Arrangements were made for me to go and visit the parish, have a look around and meet the churchwardens.

The night before my visit, I dreamed of an 'L'-shaped village, tall trees on one side of the road and open fields on the other. The church, with a fenestrated tower, was on the open side. At the extreme edge of the village, at the other end from the church, was the pub, and in my dream this was called the Board. I was being shown around by a man with a limp who was called Dick.

The village was Bilton-in-Ainsty, on the B1224 between York and Wetherby. It was right off the beaten track and I had never had reason to go there, or through it, in my life. But when I arrived I found that it was almost exactly as I had dreamt it: except the pub was called the Chequers – though it had the same sign outside it as the one in my dream – and the churchwarden who showed me round was not called Dick, but Pick – William Pick, a farmer who had a wooden leg, a replacement for the one he had lost in a shooting accident.

The small discrepancies made the experience rather more convincing than less and it seemed also to be reassuring: I mean, there is something homely and human about the fact that our occult perceptions can be as susceptible to minor errors in detail as our more mundane ones!

# 11

······

## *Only a game?*

Once there was a particularly nasty outbreak of ouija board obsession among some young people in my parish. They were youth club kids, four of them, Helen, Heather, Mike and Stuart, the youngest 15 and the oldest 17. This is just the age of burgeoning sexuality at which people seem to be most susceptible to anything connected with the occult. The two boys and two girls were friends, not paired off exactly but regular associates, and I know that their relationships were not entirely platonic.

They had got into the habit of going round to one another's houses after the club closed and on non-club nights. It was, I later came to understand, the usual scene: pop records, a bit to drink and a certain amount of cuddling up in a darkened room.

All this came to light later. The first whiff I had of there being anything amiss was when I got a telephone call from Helen's mother. Helen was the younger of the girls at 15½. She had been acting strangely and had now overdosed on her mother's valium tablets and slashed her wrists. She was recovering in the General Hospital.

I went to see her and she was able to say a few words but was barely conscious. That Sunday afternoon I went to see her parents and Mike, the elder of the boys, was with them. Helen's father said straight out, 'Michael says she was convinced she was possessed by the Devil and the only way she could get rid of it . . . him . . . was to do away with herself. And that's all I know about it except that they'd been messing with the ouija board for weeks.'

I stayed about an hour and had a very unsatisfactory conversation. Everyone was looking to everyone else for added information in order to build up a complete picture of what had been going on, but each was nervous, as if afraid to say something that would be regretted later. Mike looked particularly edgy and kept catching his breath. I suspected that he knew much more than he was saying. I got him to promise me that he and the other two who were not in hospital would not play with the ouija board again.

'I don't need to be told that, Vicar. We've all scared ourselves stiff – and now this.'

I said I would look in on Helen again in a day or two. As I got up to leave, Mike caught my sleeve. 'Can I come and see you sometime, Vicar?'

'Tonight after Evensong, if you like. Say about half past eight?'

He was on the dot. I took him into the study and gave him coffee.

'What are you doing with yourself these days?'

'I'm in the sixth form. I want to be a molecular biologist.'

'Scientists are supposed to have an interest in the occult, are they?'

'It was all an accident. That's what I've come to tell you about.'

I told him that how I might be able to help depended absolutely on his telling me the truth, the whole truth and nothing but the truth. Nothing must be left out, either to save embarrassment or for any other reason. I swore that I would say nothing to his parents or to the parents of any of the others involved. We sat there under the chiming clock and he asked me if it was all right to smoke. Then he began.

'It was just a bit of a laugh, something to do. When we first started, we all accused one another of pushing the glass and nobody really knew whether it was working or not. It got all the answers right though.'

'What sort of answers?'

'Like, "Will Stuart pass his exams?" That sort of thing. Then Stuart said he wanted to ask the glass a private question. He put it up to his mouth and held it there for a minute. Then he put it down again and we all put our fingers on again –

except Stu. He said he wanted to test it and to test whether any of us were pushing. That's why he kept his hand off.

'The glass moved really quickly, really smoothly this time and it spelt out "No." Stu laughed and said, "I thought so!"

'When we asked him what it was all about, he wouldn't tell us at first. Helen said, "What's the use in playing at all if we're going to keep secrets from one another?"

' "OK, then," said Stu. "I asked it if Heather is a virgin." Heather went bright red and hit out at him, sort of partly in fun. The rest of us just laughed.'

'So now you knew it could answer correctly independently of the touch of the person who had asked the question. What did you do next?'

'We wanted to test it again. We were excited, I suppose.'

He told me how they had asked a stream of everyday questions and received correct answers on each occasion. Then he said, 'Helen wanted us to go a lot further and ask it something we didn't know the answer to – "to see if it's really supernatural," she said.

'So she held the glass to her face and whispered, "Is there anyone there?" Nothing happened for ages and I was for giving up. Then it moved, quick and smooth like the other time. It spelt out "Captain Harry."

'We weren't sure we'd got it right. We'd been losing patience before and mucking about a bit, so Helen asked it again and this time it moved straightaway and it spelt "Old Harry."

'We were all a bit drunk by this time but it didn't matter because no one was going to come in. Heather's parents were away in Rhyl. Stuart asked it, "What does Harry look like?"

'I said, "For Christ's sake, you – sorry, Vicar – shouldn't have asked that. He might decide to appear!" But they only laughed.'

'Was there any immediate reaction – I mean, to the word "Christ"?'

'No. It didn't move for ages. Then it spelt "Sex."

'Heather said, "It must have misheard. It must have

thought Stu said, 'What does Harry like?' I mean, he can't look like sex, can he, whatever he is?"

' "OK then," she continued, and she grabbed the glass and held it over her mouth. "What else does Harry like?"

'This time it answered straightaway and spelt out "Helen's tits."

'We were laughing like anything, except Helen. She'd gone really quiet and she was pink in the face. Stu said, "It's all right, Helen. It was only a joke. No need to get all serious."

'But she was serious. She looked really – well, sexy. She was breathing hard and her sweater was . . . well, moving. We were all pretty drunk, as I told you. Then Helen just threw her sweater off, and her bra. She leaned forward, stretching over all the letters that went round the glass. Then, I suppose we had a bit of a session. We felt very sexy.'

'How were you afterwards? Were you all . . . well, your normal selves? Was Helen all right?'

'It was – '

He drew back, but I reminded him he must tell me the truth.

'It was very, you know, ecstatic. I hadn't felt anything like it before. Helen – she was right over the top. Afterwards, when I moved away from her to get a drink – a drink of water – she was all still, breathing deeply like she was in a fantastic sleep.

'We all slept for a bit and when I woke up it was really cold. The others were waking up and we tidied the place. We all had an amazing headache. We split up. Stuart went home by himself and I walked Helen home.

'It was like she was in a trance. She kept saying it was absolutely fantastic and she'd discovered something new and she was never going to let it go. She asked me if I'd enjoyed it. I said, well, I said, "Yes – it was fabulous." She said we had to do it again and again. We were only just beginning. She knew Old Harry had a lot to show us. And next time we met she was going to find out who else lived in that glass.

'She kept saying, "You know what we've done? We've discovered magic, Mike, that's what we've done!" '

He told me how their sessions become regular, twice a week

and more and, in short, how they became wilder. They discovered things to do with one another they had never imagined. But they never found anyone else in the glass except Old Harry, Captain Harry.

'Then one night, about three weeks since, we were having a session and something went badly wrong. It was pretty horrible actually. We were all together and suddenly without any warning Stuart started to be sick. He was sick and sick and sick. It was disgusting. It put us all off, calmed us right down. Poor Stuart was green. I thought he was going to pass out. Except Helen – she hadn't calmed down. She hardly seemed to notice what was going on.

'When we'd all come round a bit and Stu had stopped being sick, I said we ought to give it a miss for a week or two. I really felt it was getting out of hand, turning nasty. Helen screamed at that. She said she wasn't going to give it a miss. Then she went all quiet and rubbed her hands like she was in a conspiracy or something. Her eyes were really staring. It didn't look like her, really it didn't. She was wild. She said, "Well, I don't care if you do decide to give it a miss. I've found out how to get in touch with Old Harry all by myself. I don't need you lot. I don't need anybody!" '

That was the last session they held together.

The lad felt guilty about what had happened. He was ashamed and disturbed. I asked him if he regarded what he had said to me as a confession – though not a formal, liturgical one. He said he was glad, really, to have got it all off his chest. I asked him to kneel down and gave him Absolution. We said the Lord's Prayer together and I made the sign of the Cross on his forehead. He seemed very relieved.

In all our discussion, in all his outpouring, he had not once volunteered any opinion as to who he thought Old Harry was. He did not need to say anything.

I went to see Stuart and Heather, separately. They did not go into so much detail, but they both agreed with Mike's account. Heather did add one more piece of information. She said, 'One night when we weren't with the boys, Helen laughed and said to me, "I don't need them. I don't need anybody. I'm having an affair with Captain Harry!" '

Both Heather and Stuart were shaken and full of remorse, like Mike, but they seemed to be getting over their experience. I knew that Helen was in much deeper. So I said prayers with Heather and Stuart and went to see Helen's parents again. I had, of course, been looking in on Helen in the hospital every day. She was conscious but sleepy; pale-faced, as if drained.

At that first meeting with Mike and with Helen's parents I had suspected the adults of holding something back. Now I had to find out what it was. Had they noticed anything strange or untoward in Helen's behaviour in the week or two before she apparently tried to kill herself?

'Well,' said her father, 'she was always an excitable girl. Highly strung. She was a bit noisier than usual, certainly, but –'

His wife interrupted him: 'Oh come on, Jim, you know what she was up to. She'd become obsessed. Sex mania, if you ask me. The sounds from her room sometimes – honestly! I ignored it the first couple of times and I told Jim to do the same. He was for going in and – I don't know what.

'In fact *I* talked to her. All she said was that it wasn't what I thought, but that she wasn't into drugs or doing anything wrong. And she'd explain everything in a little while. So we left it and actually she quietened down until – well, you know the rest.'

The next day I went to see Helen again and she looked better. She was sitting up in bed and there was some colour in her cheeks. The bandages had been removed from her wrists and there were only plasters there now.

I asked her how she was feeling and she said, 'Better – now.' Her voice sounded calm and her long black hair had been washed. She said, 'Have you been to see Heather and Stuart . . . and Mike? Then you'll know all about it.'

'I know something about it but I don't know how you managed to end up in here.'

She sat up and hugged her knees. 'I fell in love with the

'Devil and when he'd had enough of me he tried to kill me.'

'D'you really believe that?'

'Of course. It was a crazy trip but I knew what I was doing all the time.'

'Why did you go through with it – your wrists, the tablets?'

'I didn't *really* go through with it, did I?'

'It was a damn close-run thing.'

'But there was something holding me back.'

'That was God, young lady. God and the love of your family – and your friends.'

'I know that now. I haven't been lying here doing nothing all this time.'

She was ready to say some prayers. I made the sign of the Cross on her forehead and again in front of her face. I pronounced Absolution and then I read some of the Prayers for Deliverance from the old *Rituale Romanum*. We talked for a while and as I left she was on the edge of sleep.

I have lost count of the number of times I have told youngsters, and sophisticates who think they can have a bit of sport with the occult, that the ouija board is not 'only a game' – or, if it is, it is one which the Devil plays for keeps.

# 12

## Synchronicity

Is coincidence more than coincidence? We usually prefer to build our lives around the theory of cause and effect: 'If I turn on the oven, then it will get hot' and so on. Jung, however, took coincidence very seriously. He noted that in earlier ages coincidences were sometimes regarded as highly significant. There was the appearance of the star over Bethlehem at the birth of Jesus, for example, and a comet appeared when Julius Caesar died. Shakespeare refers to this event in his play *Julius Caesar*:

'When beggars die, there are no comets seen;
The heavens themselves blaze forth the death of princes.'

Jung believed that coincidences were part of what he called 'synchronicity', which, he alleged, is 'an acausal connecting principle' which is not the same as cause and effect but which operates alongside it and forms another means by which we can understand the world.

Jung's writings are filled with anecdotes about sychronicity. He recalls that he was once treating a patient who told him that she had dreamed of a sword in a scabbard; at that moment, Jung saw a scarab beetle on the side of his desk. He was greatly encouraged by such episodes, for he came to regard them as evidence that the whole universe possesses a great unity and that nothing which happens is insignificant.

Jung said that we are more likely to experience synchronicity – i.e. events happening together in time – when there is a lot of psychological energy around, 'free-floating' as he put it. This may be when we are very excited or distressed, or it may be on the occasion of some big event involving what Jung called an 'archetype' – birth or marriage or death, for example.

Synchronicitous events then may be more than 'only coincidence'; they may be coded affirmations of unity, of the fact that everything in the universe is connected with everything else – even when we cannot always see how the connection is made. 'No man is an island,' wrote John Donne.

..........

I once had a striking experience of synchronicity. After ordination in the Church of England, a new deacon is required to do further study and write 'Priest's Essays' on contemporary issues in the light of theology. This is part of Post-Ordination Training, which, of course, everyone refers to as 'potty-training'. I was placed under the supervision of the Reverend Frank Lindars, Vicar of Shadwell, on the outskirts of Leeds. My subject for the essays was 'The Problem of Evil' – a philosophical dilemma which arises out of the question of how evil comes to exist in a world created by an all-powerful, wholly good God.

Frank was a highly intelligent, intensely spiritual priest with years of experience. He was a wise man and helped me greatly. In fact he became a friend, someone I could confide in. I used to go once a week to see him in Shadwell, leafy suburb territory with curling country lanes and large Victorian houses on the north side of the city.

My problems with evil were not only philosophical and theoretical but practical. The first year after ordination is an emotional shock as you visit people, or they come to you, in all sorts of distress and you receive direct experience of all kinds of psychological and spiritual turbulence. There are nervous breakdowns among the parishioners – and sometimes among the clergy! Serious illnesses, marriage break ups, suicide attempts, bereavements and, for one reason or another, plenty of dead bodies to be disposed of. And it is fairly relentless, so the new curate often feels emotionally drained or, as a colleague once expressed it, 'suffering from chronic spiritual shock'.

Over the winter of that first year I felt I was having a particularly hard time. There was a cot-death funeral followed within a day or two by the death of a 14-year-old girl. This was very distressing, as the family were reluctant to let her go and they kept her in the front room for days with the coffin lid open. I can see it now, as it was, leaning up against the wall. Somehow that lid seemed the most macabre aspect.

The day after the funeral I went to see Frank, at about ten o'clock in the morning as usual. He said something like, 'You look terrible!' And I said something like, 'Thanks!' He knew what I had been going through and he was sympathetic. He told me how important it was, especially at such times, to stick 'bloody-mindedly', as he said, to the daily routine of morning and evening prayer. He said it was very easy to feel that you were being enveloped in a cloud of evil. That is exactly how I felt: I was sleepless, irritable and ... well, not clinically depressed, but in permanently low spirits. The Problem of Evil was proving to be more than academic.

'Come on,' said Frank, 'let's go for a walk.' We sauntered along the tree-lined lanes in the bright, crisp winter air. The sun was low and it seemed extra yellow, extra light – real migraine weather, in fact.

Frank was saying, 'Your coffin lid. Yes, it's strange how a particular image can be unbearably macabre, how it can embody something really nasty and represent it fully – like an evil version of a Sacrament. I once read such an example of the personification of evil in a novel. It was *Under the Sun of Satan* by George Bernanos.

'The image, in the novel, was of a lithe, handsome boy coming round a corner leading a horse. The boy was exceptional in his looks, with electric blue eyes and long yellow hair...'

Even as Frank spoke, I heard a sound. When I looked up, there, coming round the corner, was a boy with electric blue eyes and long yellow hair. He was leading a horse.

Synchronicity or only a coincidence?

# 13

## *Tragedy with violets*

It is well known that poltergeist phenomena typically occur when there is a teenage girl in a household, but are there any certain methods by which we can tell whether a psychic or supernatural presence is attached to a person or to a place?

There was a house by the high wall of a cemetery in Leeds and the family who lived there began to suffer the unwelcome attention of a ghost.

'We should never have moved in,' said Mrs Doris Ramsden. 'I knew there was something wrong when we came to look round. It felt, well, sad – as if some great unhappiness had happened. But Jim said I was over-reacting. And it's a nice house, roomy and near for his work and all the rest. But I should have stuck out, I know I should, and followed my feeling. But they just laughed at me, the rest. And I let them talk me into it.'

'The rest' were Jim, who owned a lock-up bike shop in Stanningley Road, and their children, Trevor, aged 9, and Denise, 14. At first the happenings had intrigued them, even amused them: lights switching themselves on and off, doors slamming, things being inexplicably 'moved'. 'But,' said Jim later, 'they were only warming up exercises for what happened next.'

What happened next was that Denise saw something. She was upstairs in the bathroom, which was at the end of a corridor leading to the stairs. 'I heard somebody walking along the corridor towards me – about seven or eight paces. I thought it was Mum. Then whoever it was stopped outside the door. I shouted that I wouldn't be a minute, but there was no answer, so I guessed it was Trev mucking about.

'I pulled the door open quickly to catch him, but there was nobody there. That was a bit scary – what with all the noises and things we'd been hearing in the house. But I thought I must have been mistaken, or whoever it was had gone away. It was the middle of the afternoon, so I wasn't too scared.

'I went out of the bathroom and walked down the corridor to the top of the steps. Something brushed past me and that did scare me! I didn't see anything though till I got to the top of the stairs. I had to turn round – I thought, "I'll just take a quick look." That was when I saw a woman going into the bathroom. She turned round and gave me one of those looks that go right through you. Then she walked right through the closed bathroom door and vanished.'

'Denise screamed,' said Jim, 'and I wondered what the hell was the matter. Anyhow, I ran up and into the bathroom and there was nothing there.'

Over a period of months they all saw the woman, though Denise said she did not believe that Trevor had seen her: 'He doesn't want to be the only one who hasn't seen her. But the woman he says he saw looks absolutely different from what me and Mum and Dad have seen.'

There followed noises in the night, pots and pans in the kitchen being thrown about and things broken. Then each member of the family became ill in a different way: Jim had an upset stomach and had to shut the shop for a week; Doris got violent headaches, which she had never had before and which, she said, always came on shortly before the woman made one of her appearances; Trevor developed a cough, which, however, his mother said was 'only nerves'; and Denise suffered from cramps.

'The last straw,' said Doris, 'was when I was in the house on my own one afternoon. I'd just made myself a cup of tea and I was sitting down for five minutes to look at one of those "something and nothing" afternoon programmes on TV. Then I saw her. She was sitting there on the sofa. I just thought I saw something out of the corner of my eye, then, when I turned and looked, I nearly died!'

I asked Doris if she could recall anything about the woman's features. She said, 'She looks sad. Yes, she's definitely sad. And when she appears there's always a smell of violets. The others will tell you that as well.'

The sofa appearance was the last straw, as Doris had said, and not long after that the Ramsdens moved house. I met them all together once more before they left and my impression was of a family worn out. They did not seem to have been terrified by the appearances so much as depressed by them. And the constant, niggling minor illnesses wore away at their energy and patience. Denise could not sleep and Trevor was causing disquiet at school with his strange stories.

I said prayers with the family and blessed the house, as indeed I had done before. Each time there was a lull in ghostly activity, only for it to return later. I did mention to Jim and Doris that the manifestations might have something to do with Denise – at least the unruly pots and pans might – and in that case it was possible they would be troubled even if they did move. But by that time they had had enough and I think they were determined to move, hoping that any change would be for the better.

The new people who came in were a retired couple with a St Bernard dog. They stayed for only about 18 months before they accepted an invitation to go and live with their daughter and family in Exeter. As they told me, in all the time they were there they suffered no disturbances of any sort. Harry said, 'If there was 'owt at all, Prince would have let us know all right.' And I believed him!

So perhaps the manifestations had had some emotional or spiritual connection with young Denise?

There was a six months gap before the new occupants arrived but, once they were there, disturbances began straightaway. This family, the Meadowcrofts, was an almost exact replica of the Ramsdens. Steve and Margaret had two children: Lucy, aged 15, and Derek, aged ten. They suffered the same unruly crockery and saw the mysterious woman – once again on the corridor leading to the bathroom and in the living-room. I said more prayers and again the activity subsided temporarily, but it never went away entirely.

I decided to try to find out if anyone knew who the ghost might have been. The Ramsdens and the Meadowcrofts were agreed that the figure they saw was aged about 22 to 25 and wore 'old-fashioned clothes'. From what I could infer, these were of the Edwardian style. She was always sad.

'Makes you want to cry. Such a weight of sorrow,' said Margaret Meadowcroft. 'And always a strong smell of violets.'

Young Derek said, "Course we'll see ghosts – we live right next to the cemetery!'

I enquired of Amy Forest, who was 86 and had lived in the parish all her life, whether anything had happened in that house. She told me of a tragedy. A young woman had lived there with her husband and two young children 'before the war' – that was the First World War. The husband had left her for another woman and the wife had killed her babies – drowned them in the bath – and then placed them in the corner of the cemetery, covered over by leaves. She had then drowned herself in the bathroom. 'Margaret Dunderdale, that was her name. My mother used to speak of her often. Terribly sad.'

The following day I called on the Meadowcrofts and they told me that ghostly activity was at its liveliest. I did not wish to add to their nightmares with tales of murder and suicide, so I said I had heard there had been sadness in the house and that this had involved a young woman called Margaret. I said prayers with the family for the repose of the soul of Margaret Dunderdale. As I did this, the room was filled with a strong scent of violets.

The Meadowcrofts stayed ten years and never again complained of psychic disturbances. I was left wondering why the retired couple had never been troubled. Even the enormous St Bernard had sniffed nothing. Was it the presence of youngsters in the house which disturbed the presence called Margaret Dunderdale? Had she felt more comfortable during the tenure of the old folk? And was the disturbance of pots and pans connected with Margaret or was it so-called 'poltergeist activity' linked with Denise and Lucy?

If there are rules which govern ghostly phenomena, they are not immediately recognizable as the same sort of rules which regulate our mundane lives.

# 14

........

## *Satanism in the suburbs*

Our suburban parish church usually smelt of brass polish and flowers, so that I had got to imagining that this is how heaven itself will smell. But one morning when I went in there was a stench. I could not immediately see from the west end that the altar had been interfered with, but it had, and there was a pool of urine in the sanctuary. There were marks on the stone, magical lettering and a goat's head drawn in some kind of wax. Some of the prayer books had been defaced with obscene writings.

The vestry safe was intact, at least, and I was relieved by the discovery that none of the sacred vessels had been taken or used in the performance of whatever hideous act had take place in the church during the night.

I was angry, but decided to treat the incident as an extreme example of the sort of vandalism which many parish churches were beginning to suffer in the 1970s. Perhaps I should have called the police? But I did not. All I wanted was to get the place cleaned up and to put the incident as far from my mind as possible. I cleared up the mess and felt a sense of personal violation as I did so.

In such very limited experience of that particular sort of evil as I have had, I have noticed in others as well as in myself a similar reaction: it is not terror, or even ordinary fear; it is nausea. When I had finished I walked out into the churchyard and I was almost sick. But I went back inside and walked the length and breadth of the building, up and down the aisle, across the chancel and back again into the baptistry. It was a sickness like despair. I prayed fervently that God would rehallow the place and give me heart and encourage me again.

I sat in the church for a while in my own priest's stall and contemplated the event, tried to accommodate it as a prelude

to the bigger task of trying to forget it. The one thought at the
very front of my mind was the rightness of St Thomas
Aquinas' judgement 'Evil is banal.' It *was* banal, the whole
spectacle, the whole sordid event. It was cheap and ugly.
'Tasteless,' I thought. 'The Devil has no taste!' I got some
relief from the conjecture.

But who had done it? Were they locals who had defiled their
own parish church or did they come in by coach – a sort of
Satanists' charabanc? We had once suffered the removal of the
cross from the Lady Chapel, but that was an ordinary act of
theft which seemed almost decent in comparison to this new
violation. The cross had even been returned – perhaps as it
was impossible to sell or maybe, I was ready to believe,
because the thief had a conscience.

I went home and had a bath, got changed and listened to
some Bach on the gramophone as I was doing so. Then I went
to call on one of the churchwardens. I said, 'Somebody's been
messing about in the church. I think we're going to have to
lock it up at nights in future.'

'Kids?'

'No. Devil-worshippers.'

Tom Claypole was in his sixties, a retired office manager, a
chap with a bit of a twinkle in his eye and a habit of pulling
folks' legs. He smiled at me as if he had been waiting for me to
say something more, to complete the joke with its punchline.

'No,' I said, 'I'm serious, Tom. It was filthy.'

He gave me a drink and we talked over whether we should
call the police after all. We thought we would not, but I said,
'What are we going to tell the people?'

'I don't think we should tell them anything. I'll tell Clarry
[the other churchwarden] and let's leave it at that – unless, of
course, Clarry thinks otherwise.'

Clarry did not think otherwise. We locked up the church
every night.

Of course, I never found out who had done it, but a few
months later there was a case reported in the newspaper of
sadomasochistic goings on in a neighbouring parish. There

had also been tales of some sort of sacrificial rites in a nearby wood. Drugs were involved and a reputable solicitor, said to have been connected with the events, was being blackmailed.

We were never troubled again, but I always noticed 'black magic in the suburbs' stories after our experience. They were all remarkably similar. You could have predicted the ingredients: 'respectable' folk, drugs, kinky sex and money as the added sleaze factor. Banal.

The discovery of the banality of these sorts of doings was to me a consolation. It made it easier to despise Satanism. I think that, in popular consciousness, perhaps encouraged by darkly romantic tales and glossy films, the Devil is a glamorous figure. He is often portrayed as a gentleman and there is also the literary precedent of elegant, aristocratic libertines like Lord Byron. This sort of evil is made very attractive in Western culture and the Satanist is often portrayed as some kind of superior person – one who dares to transgress and who does so extravagantly. It is as if there should be a grandeur to evil.

This is a lie and it is the lie which St Thomas saw through so precisely. Far from being glamorous or in any way exalted, evil is squalid, sordid and contemptible. It is not worth a sensible man's time. Satanists' actions – the type of thing they perpetrated in our church – are so preposterous as to be silly. We do right to despise evil, but this should never allow us to forget or underestimate its power.

There is another side to all this, one which even gives cause for optimism. I once heard a bishop say that even Satanism was to be preferred to the spiritless, godless secularism and materialism of our age. If a man worships the Devil, it means he is at least capable of worship. And in his powerful book *But Deliver Us From Evil*, John Richards quotes Prebendary Henry Cooper, speaking after his church in Bloomsbury had been desecrated by Satanists:

A seeking after the spiritual and the supernatural – even if it can be very evil and very perverted – is certainly not so hard and impenetrable a thing as the complacent, affluent, materialist society which is all around it.

These people, I think, are quite possibly *more* capable of conversion than many others. If you turn a crucifix upside-down, you can in fact turn it the right way up again. *Laus Deo*.

# 15

## The fortune-teller

Where is the borderline between 'a bit of fun' and 'dangerous dabbling in the occult'? There were once more than a few people ready to enlighten me on this issue. When I was a country parson, I was asked if I would allow a fortune-teller at the church's garden party. It turned out that one of my predecessors had banned this popular attraction. In fact he had tried to prohibit everything that might smack of idle pleasure, including bottles of sherry as whist prizes and a Christmas raffle. I imagine that a sentence to make him run for the monastery tearing his hair out would be: 'I bet you a pint of bitter that Pilgrims Progress will win the 2.30 at Brighton tomorrow!'

Anyhow, I decided to put on a brave face against all the accusations of occultism and allow Mrs Crawford to set up her fortune-teller's tent. I even purchased a consultation myself: 'You will go over water this year and learn something you didn't know before. And, as to character, you are the sort of person who often finds himself engaged in many different tasks at the same time...' To which my reply might have been, 'Try arranging a garden party, conducting wedding interviews, compiling the diocesan returns and remembering to pick up something for tea all in one afternoon!'

It was one of those summer Saturdays which feature horizontal drizzle in a howling gale, so we reverted to Plan Two and held the event inside the Grange. But Mrs Crawford's husband and his pals had gone to all the trouble of pitching the fortune-teller's tent on the lawn and so that was where she set out her stall, gale or no gale. All luminous stripes and flapping canvas, it was like an abandoned Punch and Judy show on a deserted beach. There was a steady flow of raincoated and umbrella-carrying customers.

I was balancing a cup of tea, a book of tombola tickets and a toffee apple when I noticed two formidable ladies bearing down on me. 'If you have a minute, Vicar, we'd like a word.'

It was request that chilled the blood. There was so much unattached and violent emotion in their demeanour that I knew it would be more than one word which they were anxious to speak to me. I knew them: Sally Carruthers in the Harold Wilson-style raincoat and with one eye that wandered, and Jean Stevens, plump and made-up to look apoplectic. It was she who spoke first.

'We don't approve. It's providing a way in for Satan.'

'Fancy,' chipped in her partner, 'allowing such goings on at a *church* garden fête!'

It was no use pretending I didn't know what they were referring to, as I went for the full frontal defence. 'I must disagree with you. I think you're over-reacting. Really Mrs Crawford is quite harmless and her readings are so stylized and generalized as to be virtually meaningless. It's meant to be a bit of fun and that's how everybody takes it.'

'Not *everybody*, Vicar.'

'Well, *almost* everybody.'

People were beginning to stare and stop what they were doing.

'If you won't do something about it, we'll write and complain to the Bishop!' said – screamed – Jean, who by this time would have looked apoplectic even without the make-up.

I shuffled and edged them out into the corridor. 'Please – I wish you wouldn't make a fuss in public. You could come and talk to me afterwards.'

'But it's now we want it stopped.'

'Ought never to have been started,' added the other.

I said, 'There is absolutely nothing wrong with the enter-tainment which Mrs Crawford is providing. It's just a popular way of raising a bit of money for church funds.'

'It's like taking money from Satan!'

The fortune-teller might have diagnosed my short-temper

in her character reading. I was incensed by the stridency of the women, the absurdity of their accusation. I said, 'Don't you think you might be going just a little way over the top – "Satan" and all that stuff? It's just a joke. Entertainment and nothing more. Louie Crawford isn't telling them anything I couldn't tell them myself.'

'So we can expect to see you in the tent next year, can we, Vicar?'

'I'm sorry,' I said, 'but I just can't take this sort of thing seriously. But if you do want to come and talk to me afterwards, you know where you can find me. Now don't let's spoil a nice afternoon.'

With snorts and great holy harrumphing they made off.

I decided to pre-empt their visitation by going round to see them both on the following Monday. Washday and the wind still blowing. I was lucky to catch them both together having coffee. Never did the saying about 'two birds with one stone' carry more resonance. They had calmed down rather. I said that I agreed it was wrong to pretend serious, detailed knowledge of the future derived by occult means. Of course I was against such a practice. But I added that what Louie Crawford had been doing was not that at all. She had just been making general remarks about individual characters, stroking their egos – 'You have the habits of a perfectionist', that kind of thing.

'Have another scone, Vicar.' I think they were reassured, but as much by my visit as a social call as by anything I might have said. They did not intend to trouble the Bishop.

The matter was closed, but it was reopened the following January at the meeting of the Parochial Church Council traditionally set aside to deal with plans for fundraising events in the coming year. The Hon. Treas. passed round photocopies of the accounts for the previous year's garden party and, on the basis of these, highly theological discussions broke out over whether we should have fancy dress or a beauty contest; a raffle or a tombola or both. 'Of course,' said the PCC Secretary, 'we must have the fortune-teller again. She raised over £100 last time.' All agreed, and I took it upon myself to ask Louie Crawford if she would pitch the old stripey tent once more.

She lived in a stone house next to a disused windmill. There was always a smell of fresh-baked bread about the place.

'I can guess what you've come for.'

'Only a guess, Louie? I thought you had privileged insight.'

'Don't say that, Peter!' She looked severe. 'Well, I'm afraid the answer's no.'

'Will you be away or something?'

'No. Fred and I will be here as usual. He retires in March, you know. But I just don't want to get involved again after what happened last year.'

'Nothing happened. I went and had a quiet chat to the people who complained and that was that.'

'I wasn't meaning Sally and Jean. This is more serious.'

'You mean *you* had complaints I don't know about?'

'I've had no complaints. That's just it.'

We sat in the small back kitchen and drank tea out of a tiny china set. It was like being in an exquisite dolls' house. Louie lit a cigarette and fiddled with the ends of her hair.

'Look, Caroline Blakey died last October, didn't she?'

'Oh please God,' I thought, 'she's not going to say she *told* her she was going to die!'

'Well, I saw that death. How old was she? Thirty-six. She came into my tent all bubbly, talkative like she always is – was – and she said, "Now, Madame X, tell me the worst!"

' 'Course she knew it was me under the funny clothes. I don't think anybody came that day who didn't know it was me. I let her cut the cards, then I spread them out. There it was, clear as day, death. It was her death, I knew it. And it would be sudden and soon.

'It wasn't just the cards, Peter – though I've never seen a more fateful hand. It doesn't have to mean death, even so. There are other interpretations you can put on it. But not this time. I was absolutely certain Caroline was going to die. It was like a blast of cold air in my face.'

I could think of nothing to say.

Louie continued, 'It's frightened me, Peter. I'd been meaning to talk to you about it, but I couldn't bring myself to. The thing is, I don't know anything at all about telling the future – never have done. It's a party game, tricks I've picked up from little books that are not even half serious.

'But this was serious. I've never been more sure of anything in my whole life but that Caroline Blakey was going to die – and soon. I can't tell you how I feel – I feel ... *responsible*. What I want to know is why did it happen to *me*? *How* did I know?'

If Jean Stevens or Sally Carruthers had been there, there would have been an answer at once: 'Simple: you opened a door and the Devil walked right in!'

'Whatever else you feel, Louie,' I said, 'you mustn't start feeling responsible for Caroline's death.'

' "Start"? That's a good one! I've felt responsible ever since it happened.'

'But it wasn't your fault, don't you see? The messenger isn't responsible for the content of the message. It's not as if you told her she was going to die. It's not a curse. It's not like voodoo.'

She stubbed out her cigarette and lit another. 'I think that if I hadn't had that feeling then and there on that day, Caroline would be still be alive.'

'The doctors would tell a different tale. She died of cancer.'

'It doesn't matter what she died of. I *knew*, I tell you. And that's what worries me.'

She told me it was the one and only time in her life that anything like this had happened. That was why she felt safe giving fortune readings, because she was convinced there was absolutely nothing in it. It was a party trick and that was all.

Fred came in and he knew what we had been talking about. He said, 'When she gives me that queer look, I ask her if she's been getting any messages about me!'

'Fred! It's no joking matter!'

'Well, you shouldn't go messing around with what you don't understand,' he replied.

It was not meant cruelly, but Louie winced. She knew she had trespassed and there was no need for Fred to remind her.

'Well, now I've told you. And I'm not going to get mixed up with anything like that again – ever.'

'She means it an' all, Vicar. She's burned the pack of cards.'

I came away from their house wondering whether skill in foretelling was like skill in any other art in that it came by practice? Was it like practising the piano, say? You can't play that piece; you can't and you can't. Then one day you can. Was it simply that Louie Crawford had gone through the motions so many times that at last the motions connected with something?

St Augustine says it is like that with virtue: you practise and practise being good; you pretend. Then, one day, goodness becomes natural. I was grateful for one thing: the accidental success, or whatever it was, had not seduced Louie into becoming a devotee – as many would have been seduced.

We did not engage a fortune-teller for that year's garden party.

# 16

## He's been here before

I went into Bolton General Hospital once to visit a boy, aged nine, who had been very badly burned in a road accident. Simon was in a ward by himself and under intensive care. Although the temperature in his room was 80°, he still complained of the cold, but he was astonishingly cheerful. . . His face had been almost burned away.

The nurse showed me to his bedside and spoke to me in that deliberate, overemphatic style that told me the words were intended for Simon's ears also: 'He's so brave, Vicar. And he can sing Beatles songs – "I Want to Hold your Hand".' It was the era of the Mersey Sound.

Simon was not expected to live.

His mother had died while he was still a baby and his father had never remarried. I first saw him in Simon's ward, leaning forward in his chair staring at his own huge hands as if trying to read runes, while Simon stirred and drifted in and out of sleep. Simon was sedated for most of the time. I never heard him sing, but he said hello to me.

Brian, his father, worked at Plaistow's Packing Company on the Manchester Road and I offered him a lift home one evening after we had both visited Simon. It was autumn and Bolton was all swirling fog and bilious street lighting. We paused at some traffic lights and Brian said, 'It's my fault. They've warned me he's going to die. Sixty per cent burns, they said, it's life-threatening. It sounds so matter of fact. But I can't live with it, Peter.'

I told him more of what he knew already: that the doctors had not given up hope, that everything possible was being done and that it had been an accident; he mustn't blame himself. Yet how empty my words sounded, even to myself, just misty nothings trailing out of my mouth and mingling with the fog.

'Of course I blame myself! I'm bound to. I swerved to the right and the van smashed into us on Simon's side. I got away scot free – look at me!'

He held out his big hands in front of him. He was weary with grief and recrimination.

Simon did die a few days later. Brian and his sister, three grandparents and Simon's class teacher arrived at the crematorium on a day of slanting sunshine and hard frost. The nurse who had admired the young chap's attempts at 'I Want to Hold your Hand' came too. It was such a perfect, motionless, golden day that time itself seemed to be held in suspension. 'It's so cruel,' said the sister, 'for Brian, I mean. He loved that boy. There was nothing he wouldn't do for him . . . used to call him "my sunshine".'

We went to the Royal Hotel after the service, to a back room, plainly decorated, where food had been set out so neatly that it looked like a demonstration. Brian stared out of the wide windows and over the tidy lawns which sloped down to the stream. 'Simon would be running around out there inside two minutes. I'd have to be shouting at him not to get his best shoes mucky in that water.'

Such sad, surreal things are always said at funerals: the mental picture of a lad running about at his own wake!

When I called to see Brian a few days later, he was sitting at the kitchen table with a glass of beer, smoking a cigarette. There was a bottle of yellow pills beside the beer can. 'Doc Porter gave me these, said they'd calm me down a bit. Well, I'm calm enough. I'm having a bit of time off. There were a few days due to me in any case.'

He offered me a beer. 'I'll show you something when we've had this.' He opened another can for himself.

Afterwards he took me upstairs to Simon's room. It was full of flowers and pictures of the Beatles. Simon's last school photograph, much enlarged, had been hung over the bed. His books and boxes of toys and games were precisely set out on the long table under the window. 'Never a night went by without I came in and read to him for half an hour at bedtime.

Often I'd start by reading, but then we'd just chat – about anything. Bolton Wanderers. We'd no secrets. He could talk to me that lad, and he knew it. He was grown up for his age. Our Sheila used to say, "He's been here before, that one." '

The few days which Brian took off stretched into weeks. I went to see him some afternoons. He was unkempt and the house felt cold and damp. There were piles of unopened newspapers and the kitchen looked unvisited. I could see him losing his contact with the world, losing his confidence and disappearing into a half life of pills and cans of lager.

'You've got to look after yourself, Brian.'

'Why?'

'Because Simon would expect you to. He was proud of his dad. He wouldn't like to see you moping about like this, not taking care.'

He tapped another stub into the full ashtray. 'When Sheila died, I was devastated, I thought I'd never cope. But Simon kept me going, see. I had to stir myself and look after him. Now he's gone as well, there's nothing left – no point.'

'You've had more than your share, I'll grant you. But you mustn't just keel over now. Neither Sheila nor Simon would want you to do that.'

'You don't understand, Peter. There's nothing left. My family were my life. I worked for them. I saw everything I did as for their benefit and I got a tremendous buzz out of that. Now they've been taken from me, haven't they? There's no reason to do anything anymore.'

'You'll think I'm being harsh, but there is some reason: there's their memory. You must preserve that. It'll take courage – the everyday sort, the hardest sort, the sort that takes you into Plaistow's and makes you pick up something to cook for your tea on the way home.'

'Home? I don't know what it means any longer.'

Then one day I was on my bike and I saw him walking into Plaistow's for the afternoon shift. I visited him at home, in the morning, a few days after that and saw that the place was better looked after. It was not warm or welcoming – it hardly seemed lived-in – but it was clean and the ashtrays had been emptied; there was bacon and bread in the kitchen. I knew also that I was in the presence of acts of stoicism on the grand scale.

Brian had picked himself up by his own bootstraps and poured himself into the daily routine. He had chiselled out a portion of dignity for himself and had done it all by himself. It was very moving to see. I saw him occasionally in the months that followed and he seemed calm and determined, as if he had simply allowed himself to be governed by the ordinary routines of daily life. He was a man making the best of it. At the very least, his life was a powerful example.

About a year later he came to see me and announced that he was leaving Plaistow's and Bolton. He had met someone else and they were going to get married and open a boarding-house in Blackpool.

He said, 'You know, what hurt most about Simon's accident was that it so disfigured him. He was unrecognizable. After he'd died, I couldn't help seeing him like that. It was horrible. I couldn't imagine him how he had been. I prayed to see him like that. But I never did see him.

'Until last week. I was in the garden with Val. We were laughing about something and I happened to look up, towards the corner where Simon always had his den. And there he was, clambering about. He was laughing as well. And his face, it was all right – that cheeky monkey look that he used to have.

'He was laughing so much, Peter. You should have seen him laughing!'

# 17

## *Familiar spirits*

*The Turn of the Screw* by Henry James has been called 'the most harrowing ghost story of them all'. It is the one about two possessed children who haunt their governess and it has been made into an atmospheric film and set as an opera by Benjamin Britten.

But were the children possessed, or was it all in the mind of the governess? Can we always tell the difference between what we imagine and what is real? Some would go further and ask what we mean by 'real' anyhow. I knew a man, a tenor in our church choir, who told me he had seen ghosts all his life. Really, he was so used to them and he talked about them with such nonchalance that they might have been ordinary next-door neighbours or workmates.

There is an old saying in religious circles to the effect that one should not become too familiar with holy things – vestments, crosses, chalices and the like. I think perhaps the same might be made to apply to supernatural things. There is something wearing about the sort of spiritualist talk which recounts a ghostly visitation in such words as, 'Old Fred turned up again last night.' It does not sound quite right, I think, to speak as if one were on nodding terms with mysteries.

Clive the choirman was a bit like that. Ghosts would appear, according to him, in his front room and warn him not to take the A1 to Doncaster the following day because there was going to be an accident which would block the road near Barnsley. Or, if there was a death in this family, the ghostly clan would gather round Clive's bed and solemnly announce that Annie (or whoever) was being 'welcomed home'. To hear Clive talk was to gain the impression that the whole realm of the supernatural was called into being to supply him with inside gen about anything from the date of Armageddon to which roadworks to avoid on the way to Hull.

A bachelor, he would always appear in the vestry for Matins – half an hour ahead of everyone else – wearing a knowing conspiratorial look. It was as if he believed that I, by my vocation and profession, and he, by his occult privilege, shared access to a whole world of experience denied to everyone else, certainly to mere members of the choir. He would robe and stand looking out over the graveyard as a child looks at a fairground, itching, as it were, to be in the thick of it. Before long he would say, 'Have you ever *seen* anything about the church, Vicar?' You felt like saying, 'Oh yes. Pews, hymn books, Bibles, a pair of glasses somebody left behind. . .'

It did not matter how many times Clive had asked the question before, it was always as if I had never answered it. His talk would run on, 'Last night I was sitting by myself watching the late night news. Emily had gone up to bed [Emily, his sister, had always "gone up to bed" or "just popped out"] when I smelt a familiar smell.'

Of course, it turned out to be Aunt Edith, departed this life, who when she was living had kept a rose garden. Or, if it wasn't Aunt Edith, it was some old pal from RAF days come to chat about the price of cigarettes. Or his twin brother who had died when he was 18 months old, 'Before he could talk. But he always talks to me now, you know.' I bet he does!

It is often feared that youngsters will get drawn into involvement with the supernatural because it is so fascinating. They should be introduced to Clive: they would be bored stiff. Well, that is not likely now, because he is dead himself. Perhaps *he* appears smelling of roses or St Bruno pipe tobacco and spoils someone else's perusal of the late night news?

But the last story he told me, only a month or so before he died, was different. He was ill in bed and I went to visit him. I can remember thinking, as I walked to his house knowing very well that he was not long for this earth, that of all people he must be contemplating the prospect of dying fairly cheerfully. So many spirits had visited him that his death would be merely a return visit!

Clive looked ill. His face was battleship colour and lined like a cracked pavement. He had always been a big, bluff fellow, as you might expect of one who showed every sign of being at home in this world and with the inhabitants of the next. But when I visited him that day he looked uncertain and withdrawn, almost cringing.

'Sit in the easy chair, Vicar. I want to tell you a story.'

It seemed from his tone that he was going to recount the latest of his visitations. But he said, 'I've just had the most appalling experience. I thought I would die of fright.'

Clive afraid of ghosts? It was as if a lion-tamer should take fright at a cat.

'Look, last Tuesday night I woke up. It was the early hours – about two o'clock, if that. Over there in that chair there was the most horrible crone I have ever seen. You know when you read about the Gorgon when you're a boy? Well, she was worse.

'Her face was moving constantly in a cackle, but there was no sound. And she was luminous, a horrible yellow light. It was evil and nothing else. She seemed to be saying, "I'm here at last, Clive. All the friendly ghosts were imposters, but I'm the real thing!"

'I was shaking. I nearly passed out. Instinctively I pulled the covers over my head. I lay there panting for hours. I think I must have dropped off into a doze eventually, but it was only filled with nightmares. Well, I could see through the bedclothes that it was getting light, then the sun came up and filled the room, so I felt calmer. It had been a bad dream and now it was over. I mean, I'd never seen anything like that before in all my experience.

'When I threw back the covers there she was, sitting where you're sitting, 18 inches in front of my face. I cried out and she really seemed to enjoy that. Then she vanished.'

I felt uneasy, sitting in the Gorgon's chair. I asked Clive if he had seen her again. 'Oh no, thank God! I don't know what I'd do if I did. I told the nurse when she came in, but she only said that it was my illness making me a bit vulnerable. Vulnerable! I tell you, anybody would feel vulnerable if they saw *that thing*.

'Will you say a prayer, Vicar – that she won't come back? I feel I ought to be asking you for an exorcism.'

'Of course. And I'll do better than that. I'll come again tomorrow and bring you Holy Communion.'

Clive seemed brighter for having got the awful experience off his chest and he talked some more – and not, for the first time in my recollection, about ghosts.

'You know, I wish I'd married. I did have the chance once, but it was the war and I had to go away and . . . well, things change.'

'Yes, Clive, things changed like that for a lot of men and women of your generation.'

He was much improved in spirits the next day when I took him the Sacrament. When the ritual was over, the home help brought in some coffee. Clive said, 'What I was on about yesterday, not marrying and all that. I sometimes think that all my ghostly visitors came in lieu of blood relatives, as a sort of consolation prize for not having a wife and children of my own.

'And the nasty piece of work I saw the other night – I reckon she must be the black sheep of the family!'

# 18

## Like a little candle

How much trust can you put in tales told by young children?

There was a child, Zoë, who lived with her parents in the suburban parish where I worked as a curate when I was newly ordained. Zoë was a twin but she had lost her sister, Alice, in a car accident at the age of three.

The family could not get over the tragedy. Alan, Zoë's father, worked in a shoe shop in the middle of Bradford. I did not know him before the accident but everyone said he had been a jovial, easy-going sort with a penchant for practical jokes. After the death of his daughter, however, he had become morose and taciturn, turned in on himself, 'with hardly,' as his wife Jean said to me one day, 'a word for the cat.'

They were not regular churchgoers but I visited them, as my predecessor, who had conducted Alice's funeral, had done. They grieved deeply even three years after the accident and the house was unnaturally quiet – restrained, as it were – and Zoë was always being shushed. I was apprehensive about her upbringing. She was pale and reticent and life did not seem to be much fun for her.

There were photographs of the sisters together all over the house but none of Zoë alone after Alice's death. The conversation of Alan and Jean, after Zoë had gone to bed, was all gloomy reminiscence: 'We thought we had everything, didn't we, Jean? We called them Alice and Zoë – "A" to "Z", you see – because they were the beginning and the end to us; the be-all and end-all.'

'Zoë still is, isn't she?' I would try to say and they would shower me with, 'Oh yes, of course.' But then everything would go quiet and Alan would pour another drink. He had not taken to the whisky in a big way exactly, but I could see it was getting to be a standby. It was hard to dislodge them from their distress.

Then one day when I called they were jumping for joy: 'Guess what? Jean's expecting. July. Zoë's absolutely thrilled. Well, we all are.'

The child was born right on time and I performed the christening in the church at the end of August: Anne-Marie, a sister for Zoë, now aged six.

I followed up the christening with a visit a couple of weeks later. Alan was at work and Zoë was at school, so I had the chance to talk to Jean on her own while the baby slept. She had always blamed herself for Alice's death. She had been taking the twins to the playgroup when Alice had 'run off, just like that, right into the road. She'd never done anything like it before. But I'll always accuse myself. She'd been naughty that morning over her breakfast and I gave her a smack – not much, not enough to hurt really, just to bring her up sharpish.

'Well, she went and threw a tantrum and I reckon she was still a bit out of sorts when we set off for the playgroup. In fact I know she was. But I thought best to carry on as normal. What else can you do? I know now I should have kept her at home that day and it never would have happened.'

I had heard the story before, of course, and I was hoping that this might be the last time she would feel the need to tell it. Indeed, as the weeks went by and Anne-Marie thrived, it did begin to seem as if the whole family was throwing off the old despair. But then there was another tragedy: Anne-Marie died – a cot death. The horrible unfairness of it, the one family suffering so much awfulness – there was nothing that could be said.

Eight months after the baptism, there I was conducting the funeral. It was a wild March day, the churchyard full of daffodils hysterical in the gale, the undertaker carrying the tiny coffin in front of him up the path from the lychgate, and behind him, looking so frail with distress that I thought they would fall over, Alan and Jean in black. Zoë had been kept away but the organist played, by request, a Sunday school hymn:

Jesus bids us shine with a pure, clear light
Like a little candle shining in the night,
In this world of darkness we must shine –
You in your small corner and I in mine.

No one sang. There were only Alan and Jean in the congregation in any case, except for the undertaker and his driver, who stood throughout behind the glass doors at the end of the nave. The church seemed ridiculously large and the rafters groaned in the high wind. The parents did not want to go on to the crematorium, so I said the whole service in the church except the bare words of committal. I sat in the funeral car with the absurd little coffin across my knees.

Surprisingly, Alan and Jean did not seem to fall into deep grief again. It was almost as if they were determined not to this time. They went out together as a family, more than they had ever done.

I was at their house one evening in the autumn following Anne-Marie's death. They showed me photographs from a holiday in the Algarve and Alan opened bottles of beer. Zoë was on the floor in the corner with her drawing-book.

'I wish we could have a puppy, Daddy!'

'You know we haven't really the space for one, darling. And. . .' his voice fell away, 'we're right on the main road.'

Zoë left her book and ran across to me. 'I did have a puppy once, you know!'

The family had never owned a dog. Truth to tell, Alan was not fond of animals.

'You little . . . romancer!' said Jean, adding, 'She does make things up with a vengeance these days! She's never had a puppy. Now, tell the truth, Zoë!'

Zoë began to cry. 'I'm not making it up. I *did* have a puppy and it used to come to play with me in my bedroom. It was sitting on Anne-Marie's face the night she died.'

# 19

## The little girl by the sea

The Yorkshire coast is rich in seafaring history. Whitby and Staithes have connections with Captain Cook and between these two towns lie several remote seaside villages built into the sides of some of the most spectacular cliffs in England.

In the eighteenth and nineteenth centuries these villages were busy ports for the iron and alum mines but, since the decline of these industries, they have become quiet places where the industrial remnants have become overgrown or fallen into ruin, like the old harbour at Port Mulgrave. You can walk the cliffs or the shore for miles and come across no one. In winter, particularly when a south-east gale is blowing, there is a raw beauty about the coastline, and on a fine summer day the shore is a magical place and the view from the clifftops seems limitless.

A married couple in my parish bought a holiday cottage at Port Mulgrave and I was invited to go there by myself for a break from church work and to do some writing.

I went one autumn day and spent an hour or two walking the shore collecting fossils before settling to write in the evening. The kitchen and back bedroom looked out over the sea, while the view from the living-room and from the bedroom where I slept was of similar small houses across the steep street. You could look out and down at the many different styles of walls and roofs and windows and at the chimneys, always in use since at that time everyone had a coal fire.

It was a peaceful evening, as I recall, except for the sound of some child bouncing a ball out on the street – or so it sounded. I went to bed at about midnight, slept soundly, awoke with the gulls and made an early start back home. When I went to give in the keys, the owners of the cottage asked, 'Did you come across anything . . . untoward?'

I wondered what they could possibly mean. Rats? Mice? Blocked drains? But I was in a hurry, so I said quickly, 'No, nothing.' I left and gave no more thought to the incident.

About a month after this – yes, it was a month for I was preparing the carol services – I received an anxious phone call from the friends who had lent me the cottage. Could I go round at once? It was a matter of some urgency.

'Now, tell the Vicar what you told us and see what he makes of it all.'

The words were addressed to Brian, aged 16, the only son of the folk who owned the cottage. He was agitated and nervous and would not look straight at me. He smoked one cigarette after another as he told me his tale. In fact he would not tell me anything at first, but blushed and hesitated and turned away until he was half cajoled and half threatened into speaking by his mother, a formidable woman who stood with her arms folded throughout the long conversation.

She began, 'Now tell him, Brian. You've gone and frightened yourself, haven't you?' Then, aside to me, but still in her full, echoing tones, 'He's been up to the cottage with a couple of his mates and I think they've all had a drop too much lager. Anyhow, whatever it was that happened, it's frightened him good and proper. I've even had him to the doctor and he's been taking some tranquillizers, but look at him – still like a zombie and smoking his head off.' She added, derisorily, 'He says he's seen a ghost.'

It was a confused and confusing story, but there was the ring of truth about it simply because parts were so vivid. To begin with, Brian and his mates had been drinking.

'But we weren't drunk. Then there was this noise of somebody bouncing a ball really hard. Mike went to open the door and see what it was and there was this fantastic blast – like really cold – and Mike said there was a girl on the stairs.

'Steve and I went to look but there was nowt there. We said he'd made it up, Mike. We said he was . . . [pause while he searched for an acceptable translation of what he and Steve had said] . . . we said he was mad about girls. It's all he thinks about.

'But it was cold. Freezing. Then we looked up and saw her. It was a little girl, about nine or ten. She was coming down the stairs, smiling at us. She had a ball in her hand. Then, when she got halfway down, she just disappeared. I saw it. I'm not making it up.'

I am ashamed to say that I actually laughed out loud at this point – not because of what Brian had said, but because of the look of transcendental scepticism on his mother's face.

'It's true, Vicar. It's true. Honest!'

'What did you do then?'

'We were scared. We daren't go upstairs. We went back in the front room and shut the door. It was all quiet. After a bit we went and had another look up the stairs but we couldn't see nowt. And it wasn't cold anymore. Steve went halfway up the steps but he got scared and came down again.

'There was no way we were gonna go upstairs to sleep. We tried to sleep downstairs – on the sofa, on the rug and that. But we heard some noises again and decided to get out. We locked up and Mike drove us back here.'

'Woke us up in the middle of the night,' said his father. 'I wondered what the hell was going on.'

'Would you go back there?' I asked.

'Not bloody likely!' said Brian. His mother fixed him with a look.

'But,' said Brian's father, 'there's been another development since. We let the place to two nuns from down south who were doing a tour of the north east – Whitby Abbey, Holy Island and the rest. They didn't see anything exactly, but they had to leave in a hurry – couldn't stand being mucked about.

'They'd go for a walk on the beach and when they came back and tried to make a cup of tea they'd find that all the kitchen stuff – pans and cups and everything – had been shoved under their beds.'

His wife gave me a spooky stare. She cleared her throat and said, 'We wondered if you'd go up there and do an exorcism, Vicar?'

I explained that exorcisms were last resort tactics and that an exorcism was an official (and very long) rite used only by experts acting under the direct and specific authority of a bishop.

'Things were made a lot worse by that film *The Exorcist*. Before that, a diocese might have one case of genuine devil-possession in a decade. Now people are dabbling in the occult all over the place and scaring themselves silly. They work themselves up to imagining they're possessed and ask the Church to get involved. It's very rarely a case for the exorcist, though – just over-excitement. But people can be badly frightened.'

'You see, I told you he'd say we invented it all!'

'I'm not saying that, Brian. You've obviously had a nasty shock. I'll certainly go up to the cottage, but I don't think there'll be any need for exorcism.'

'What will you do?' asked his mother.

'I'll say a few prayers and bless the house.'

'What sort of prayers?'

'Ordinary prayers. Our Father, the Glory be to God on High. In a troubled house like that it's a good idea to say a prayer for the repose of the souls of the departed. And in a house-blessing it's customary to sprinkle each room with holy water.'

'What's holy water?'

'Water that's been blessed by a priest – like at a christening.'

'I thought it would be something special!' She sounded disappointed.

'It *is* special. But it's just holy water. It doesn't come in different octanes for different performances you know!' I explained that a house-blessing could be more elaborate, a rite in itself like a holy house-warming. 'People sometimes have them and invite their friends when they move homes. But in this case I shall simply take my flask of holy water and say some English prayers.'

..........

It was brooding December on the bare coast – the sky the colour of a dirty duster and no wind. It hardly got light all day. I put on my surplice and stole and walked from room to room: 'Absolve, O Lord, the soul of thy servant, that she who is dead to the world may live to Thee: and wipe away by Thy most merciful forgiveness whatever sins she may have committed in life through human frailty. Through Christ our Lord. Amen.'

Up the stairs and into the bedroom which overlooks the sea: 'Eternal rest grant unto her, O Lord; and let light perpetual shine upon her. Amen.'

The house was quiet. It was even cosy downstairs as I sat by the fire writing my article for the January parish magazine. But the night was disturbed. I had a nightmare, the details of which I cannot now recall, but it involved the sea and anger and departing ships. I awoke to find myself not in bed but standing at the top of the stairs in the darkness. If I had taken another step I would have fallen headlong.

I turned on the light and walked down to the kitchen. As I sat there with my coffee, I heard a rhythmical sound from upstairs, as if someone there was engaged in a game or a dance. Then there was a noise from the stairs and a child's rubber ball came bouncing into the kitchen and stopped just in front of my chair. It was perfectly solid and ordinary. I picked it up and walked back upstairs with it. All was now quiet.

In the morning I walked along the shore. A wind had got up and the atmosphere was exhilarating. Towards lunchtime I went in the Ship Inn where a few retired locals were playing dominoes at the table next to a huge coal fire. They drew me into conversation, out of a friendly mixture of kindness and curiosity, and as soon as they discovered where I was staying, one of them said, 'Have you seen her, then?'

I asked for the story.

'It were more 'n 'undred years ago. 'Er father was a seaman – bit of a pirate by all accounts. Smugglin'. 'E went out an' left 'is little girl locked in the cupboard in the bedroom. Some says 'e meant to kill 'er, but there's them as sez 'e was just so drunk 'e forgot all about 'er. When they found 'er, poor mite, she was dead. Starved.

'Everybody knows about 'er. They say she can't rest. 'As she been botherin' you, then?'

'No, she hasn't bothered me.'

I had left my clerical collar off or else I imagine I would have faced a stiffer interrogation. I lunched in the Ship and then walked back up the cobbled road to the cottage. It was sunny now and the village was all sharp shadows. I looked up at the cottages all higgledy-piggledy on the cliffside. Nothing had altered much in 100 years: fishermen and wheeling gulls, people in scarves standing on their doorsteps to catch what there was of the sunshine. It was a sleepy afternoon.

I went into the cottage and stayed another night there, in the same bedroom, the one with the tall cupboard. I heard no strange sounds, suffered no nightmares. In fact the house seemed to have fallen calm and quiet. The atmosphere was warm, benign.

In the morning I read the psalms set for the day in the *Prayer Book* and ended with *Requiem aeternum dona eis Domine, et lux perpetuam luceat eis* (Rest eternal grant unto *them*, O Lord, and let light perpetual shine upon them). Then I got in the car and drove home.

# 20

·······

## *The Doppelgänger*

We usually think that dreams are bits of nonsense that occur in the night and that they are dispelled entirely by the daybreak. But for thousands of years in our cultural and religious history, dreams were regarded as important events and full of significance for waking life. Joseph's dream of the thin cows and the fat cows is recorded in the Book of Genesis, while in the New Testament, another Joseph is informed of the birth of Christ in a dream.

Is there a language of dreams? If so, it is symbolic, in that we are unable to think, or dream, without symbols. Some psychotherapists work on the principle that there is a language of dreams which we are able to interpret and learn from.

I knew a man in my Leeds parish, Mark Shannon, who had kept his personal dream diary for 40 years. He claimed that the interpretation of these dreams was his religion and that he had received priceless emotional and moral guidance from them. Mark was fascinated by symbolism of all sorts and his house resembled a magician's parlour. He had a crystal ball and numerous packs of Tarot cards, books and videos on astrology, palmistry and clairvoyance, ghosts, demons and angelology. If he had lived in an earlier age he would have been an alchemist. As it was, he had to settle for being a chemist!

That was before he retired. After his retirement, I would visit him about once a month and his talk was always interesting. One day he said, 'Yes, the symbolism surrounding Christ is rich indeed. You know his early disciples were fishermen and they took the Greek word for fish as a code sign for their Christianity when they were under persecution. This is how it worked...'

He wrote on a piece of scrap paper:

| Ιηους | = | | = Jesus |
|-------|---|---|----------|
| Χριστος | = | | = Christ |
| Υιος | = | | = God |
| Θεου | = | | = Son |
| Σωτηρ | = | | = Saviour |

'Jesus Christ Son of God, Saviour' – all built on the letters of the Greek word ΙΧΘΥΣ, a fish. And Christ was born at the beginning of the Age of the Fish. It makes you think there's something fishy going on, doesn't it?'

Mark was amazing value, though occasionally I detected something of a charlatan in him. He liked to startle you with his constant discovery of strange coincidences and his even stranger predictions. Some of these came true, however: for example, he predicted the pulling down of the Berlin Wall to the exact year – and he made that prediction in 1981.

Finally he became very ill and was taken into Leeds General Infirmary where I went to see him. Of Mark it could truthfully be said that he was always cheerful. It was as if all his reading, his drawing of horoscopes and his dream interpretation had put him on nodding terms with the infinite. When I called on him one April day he said enthusiastically – so enthusiastically that I feared he might discourage other patients – 'I'm going to die very soon. Probably on Saturday.'

I knew better than to start saying 'Tut Tut!' and 'Of course you're not!', so instead I said, 'And what brings you to that conclusion?'

He replied, 'Oh, it won't be my *conclusion*, old boy – just another step on the ladder!'

He began to tell me a story by and about Johann Wolfgang von Goethe, the great romantic poet and novelist. 'Goethe said that to see the Doppelgänger, the very startling ghost of oneself, is to prevision one's own death. You must know the story of the horseman who went out riding in the forest one morning and the first person he saw coming towards him was his double, his Doppelgänger. He rightly understood this to be a sign of his approaching death.

'Well, old boy, I saw my Doppelgänger last night in a dream. I was walking down to the hay bridge over the river where I used to meet my lady friend long ago. Now, I always met her on a Saturday, just before one in the afternoon.

'In my dream I was on my way to the hay bridge and it was a lovely spring day. But instead of seeing Jane walking towards me, I saw me, myself! *Then* I saw Jane. It was so delightful, I was sorry to wake up. Now, what do you think of that?'

He was smiling for all his discomfort and I can truly say that neither in this instance nor in any other stories which Mark told me was there ever even the hint of anything morbid or sad.

But he did die, peacefully, on the following Saturday, just before one o'clock in the afternoon.

# 21

## *The statue*

Manston, where I was once curate, has had a disturbed history. Eighty years ago it was a village on the edge of the city on the main railway line between Leeds and Scarborough. There were mining connections and a good deal of farming there. It was a typical Yorkshire parish, down-to-earth and with no extremes, going its own way and taking little interest in national controversies.

Into this eminently normal milieu came the Reverend Charles Russell as vicar in 1919, causing an immediate sensation. For those who are not closely acquainted with the Church of England, I should say that it is a very broad church in which the whole range of belief and doctrine is represented. There are 'dancing in the aisles' evangelical and charismatic congregations and others who take reticence in worship to such a degree that, if you were to drop in on a service, you might conclude that they had fallen asleep. There are low church parishes so Protestant and anti-imagery that they do not even put candles on the altar and the only vestments worn by the minister – they will not call him 'priest' – are surplice, scarf and university hood. At the other extreme there are churches famous for their incense and elaborate ritual – 'smells and bells' – processions, candles, statues and vestments so dazzling that they would look well on a starship commander.

Charles Russell was of this last sort. He was so high church that St Peter's, Rome, would have appeared low by comparison. Naturally, he wished to see his beliefs about how church services should be ordered put into practice in Manston. Whatever the externals of worship might be to anyone else, to Russell they were not externals at all but integral, organic parts of the faith. Vestments were sacred clothes, the chalice and paten were holy vessels and the bread and wine were, by Transubstantiation, the Body and Blood of Christ.

A new vicar usually adjusts the churchmanship, high or low, of his parish gradually and marginally and so controversy is avoided. But Russell was no diplomat; he was a zealot. At once he instituted the whole paraphernalia of high church worship into the quiet and moderate congregation. Holy Communion was announced as 'Mass' and processions were introduced, along with incense, the sanctuary bell and many extra candles.

For the parishioners it was a culture shock. Perhaps they would have got used to it in time if Russell had innovated more gradually. Other parsons had done as much and got away with it. But it was not in Russell to be a gradualist.

Then he took one step too far: he purchased a large statue of the Virgin Mary and installed it in a prominent position in front of a pillar on the south side of the nave. There was uproar. The people would not stand for these 'Romish practices'. On the model of civil disobedience, they went in for 'ecclesiastical disobedience'. They disrupted services and even tripped up Father Russell – as he styled himself, but as they refused to call him – in procession. Still he persisted, believing no doubt that he was being persecuted for righteousness' sake.

Finally, one cataclysmic day, a group from the riled congregation tore down the statue of the Blessed Virgin and took themselves off to build a new church which they called The Free Church of England. They even constructed an elegant modern building not more than 100 yards from Russell's shrine. It was a sad period and generated a scandal which even attracted the attention of national newspapers.

However, Russell did not stay as Manston's vicar for very long. He left in 1925 and was succeeded by the Reverend Cesar Romeo Taglisi. The very name must have been a Papal red flag to the suburban Leeds bull! But Taglisi – 'Taglis', as he preferred to be called – was a saint. He was, it is true, high church, but his was such a conciliatory and gentle style that he began to heal the rift in the parish. He stayed for 25 years and I never heard anything of him but good.

One day in Manston I was cutting the grass at the curate's house when a parishioner called out to me. He was in great distress. I knew him only slightly, for he had been in the parish barely three months. He had moved to Leeds from Nottingham, where he had lived for 20 years with his wife. One day she had come down to breakfast and announced without any preamble that she was leaving him.

That day when I was in the garden he told me all about it: 'I'd no idea that she'd been having an affair. It had been going on for two years. I must have been stupid not to realize. She upped and left and it just broke me. I've always loved her so much. I love her still. I'd have her back tomorrow. I need her.'

I took him into the house and we had some coffee.

'I get these panic attacks, you see,' he said. 'Often it's when I'm on my own at home – especially in the night. Today's the first time it's happened while I've been outdoors. Just here, on the corner. That's why I called out for you.'

He calmed down and began to apologize for intruding. 'You must think I'm out of my mind.'

I reassured him and he said he would be on his way. He was going to start coming to church on Sundays. Prayer definitely helped, he said. 'In fact, if it's all right with you, I'll go across to church and just be quiet for a few minutes now.'

He was gone about half an hour and I was back outside cutting the grass again when suddenly, out of the corner of my eye, I saw him leaning on the gate, a smile right across his face.

'Thank you very much, Mr Mullen. I got so much help out of that. I just went and sat in the nave under the statue of the Virgin Mary. She seemed to look at me and understand. It was so comforting.'

I asked him exactly where he had been sitting and he gave me a puzzled look. 'On the south side by the fat pillar – under the statue, as I said.'

I did not tell him that we had no statue of the Virgin Mary in Manston church and we had not had one since that day in

1921 when it was wrenched from its position. But when I went across to Evensong at five o'clock, I made it my business to look. There was no statue: there were only the scars in the stonework of the pillar to show where it had once been.

# 22

## The car

Joe Elseworth had a car. It was nothing out of the ordinary, just a Ford Cortina 'H' registration 1969. When I first met Joe it was 1986 and he had recently put a new engine, a 1600, in it. He boasted to me that he had got 200,000 miles out of the previous engine: 'Y'know, I could have gone eight times round the world in her for that mileage, Vicar.'

He was not the sort of chap who had ever gone very far, though, just to work each day at the Picture Drome cinema in Leeds, where he was a commissionaire. He was a big man with a torch and a loud whisper who had spent half a lifetime shushing kids in the Saturday matinée. Now he had retired he and his wife Irene would go for a drive on Sundays, either to the coast or the Yorkshire Dales, and that was as far as he had ever driven, except for two or three times (in 40 years of marriage) when they had gone on touring holidays to Devon and North Wales.

I got to know Joe and Irene as a couple who each made out that the other was a tyrant, but it was always obvious that this was only a performance, a double act for the benefit of visitors, and that really they were very fond of each other.

They were on their drive one day when I stopped to talk to them. She said, 'You won't get *him* to come to church, if that's what you're after, Vicar. That car is his god.' He was at that moment giving his god a vigorous polish with a yellow duster.

They asked me to stay for a cup of tea and the conversation was unrelentingly automobiles. When Joe asked, 'What sort of job have you got, Vicar?', I thought at first he was asking me what it was like to be a parson, but it turned out that what he really meant was what sort of car did I drive! When I told him it was an Allegro, there followed a lot of serious talk about power-weight ratio which was mostly beyond me.

When Joe excused himself and went upstairs the topic continued to be automobiles, even in his absence, only in place of Joe telling me about the car, Irene told me about the car and Joe. 'I sometimes think, especially since he retired, that it's sent him a bit funny, that car. He spends such a lot of time on it – and in it. He'll go and sit in it – not going anywhere – for half an hour at a stretch. He says it helps him think. Goodness only knows what he thinks about!'

Joe and Irene's house was modest, a 1950s semi, but on the corner, so there was a stretch of garden front and rear. They reckoned, they told me, they would end their days there, 'unless we win the pools'.

Then they *did* win the pools – not the jackpot, but a handy few thousand pounds. They had no time to move, however, for early one morning just three weeks later, the postman found Joe dead in his car. He had sealed the garage and attached a pipe from the exhaust through the driver's window. The inquest recorded the only verdict that would fit the facts: suicide.

I went every other day to visit Irene and at first she would say nothing at all. We would sit in silence for a while and after that she would bow her head while I said the Lord's Prayer and a blessing; then I would leave. After a few weeks she began to speak a little, but slowly in a low voice. I remembered her as an easy-going ebullient woman with an unmistakable laugh, but now she moved as if she were trying to leave no evidence of her existence. Having no children, she was without close family. The neighbours kept an eye on her, but I was worried because Joe's death had knocked the life out of her as well.

Early one morning I was shaving when the telephone rang. It was Irene.

'I know it's only six o'clock and I'm sorry to bother you, but I wanted to catch you before you go across to church. Say a prayer for Joe, will you please? And say one for me. . .' Her voice trailed off and she broke down. I could hear her sobs as if they were coming from miles away, from some terrible, lost place. I said I would go round at once. Pulling on my coat and scarf, I stepped out into the snow. Over the church there was a huge fuzzy moon like a bright light behind a curtain.

Most of the houses in the suburb were in darkness but from a good way off I saw Irene's lights. Her curtains were open so I could see her inside, pacing. She was holding a cigarette. She looked like a corpse. Her sparse hair stuck out in all directions and there were grey streaks down her face. The cigarette was not even lit. I suppose that, staring out of the lighted room, she could see only its reflection, and I had to ring the doorbell.

'I've made a pot of tea,' she said. 'Will you sit down five minutes?' She sounded calmer.

She brought the tea and poured it, then, bethinking herself, offered me a cigarette and lit her own. 'I've been meaning to ask you something, Vicar. I want you to get rid of that bloody car for me. Will you do it? Will you? Say you will.'

I reassured her and she was calm again, though it was unnerving to look at her because she really did have a haunted expression. Her eyes were wide and sort of . . . knowing.

'I'd better tell you the whole tale,' she said.

'You know how fond Joe was of that damn car, mending it, polishing it? I used to say he took more care of the car than ever he took of me. But I didn't mean it. He knew I didn't mean it. It was just a joke. But, you know, he was obsessed, besotted. He took to going and sitting in it for an hour at a time – longer some days.

'Then he came in one afternoon and said something that made me think he'd snapped, you know, gone off his rocker. He said, "Irene, I can talk to that car. And what's more, the car talks back to me. She" – *she* mind you! – "she tells me things."

'I made some daft remark. You know – I was trying to humour him. To tell the truth, I didn't know what to say. I couldn't say I thought he was talking like he was two sandwiches short of a picnic, could I?

' "And," he went on, "if I ask her questions, she answers me!"

'So I said – I suppose it just slipped out – "Ask her to give you t'numbers that'll win pools!"

'He didn't say anything and I knew I'd offended him. He just looked. Then he walked away.

'I tried to put the whole silly business right out of my head – just forget it ever happened, like. Then a week or so later Joe came to me with something written down on a bit of paper. "There you are," he said. "That's winning numbers for next week!"

'He'd got 'em, as he said, from her – from the bloody car! I couldn't think. I said, "Well, you'd better send 'em in then, hadn't you?"

' "Don't you worry," he said, "that's just what I'm going to do."

'*You* know what happened, Vicar: we won. I told myself – I told Joe as well – it was just a fluke. What else could it be? But then things started to get really nasty. Joe began telling me things, things about myself I'd never told him. Things that happened when I was a little girl. Oh, nothing wrong – but detail. It was like having my life run in front of me like a film. Where was he getting it from?

'I told him he'd got to stop. I said it wasn't right – not healthy. But he only grinned and spent more time in the blasted car than ever. That's why I feel so guilty. I should've stopped him in his tracks. I should've phoned you, Vicar. But frankly, I was annoyed. It was a queer going on, I'll tell you. I felt as if I was living with a lunatic – but a devil, you know, who could tell you things.'

She lit another cigarette from the stub of the first one, coughed as she inhaled and pulled the cord on her dressing-gown tighter. Then she let out such an awful wail I thought the neighbours would rush in to see who was throttling her: 'Oh, I should have stopped him! It had gone too far!'

She fell quiet again and told me the rest in a haunted whisper.

'One night he said the car had told him that it – she! – knew everything. He said, "My destiny is tied up with that car, Renée. There's a hidden purpose and tonight I'm going to be told what it is." That was the night we found him!'

After that hints came out, bits of information from Joe's past. He had suffered some mental disturbance when he was younger and there had been the suspicion of schizophrenia. But he had lived for 25 years without any more trouble. Certainly the car episode had the classic signs: paranoia, delusions, voices, secrecy and the rest. There was no doubting the fact that the balance of his mind was disturbed.

No doubt also the pools forecast was a coincidence?

I promised I would help Irene to get rid of the car. I thought it over as I walked back to the Vicarage in the red morning light. Should I say exorcising prayers in it first?

In the end there was no need, and no need to try to sell it either. That night, Irene set fire to it.

*Of further interest...*

# Families are Forever
*True stories of encounters beyond the grave*

CASSANDRA EASON

Family ties are not of this lifetime only but can survive death and continue to provide us with love and joy, strength and reassurance. This is the message of *Families are Forever*, which describes the encounters of real people with loved ones they thought they had lost forever. Through words, gestures, jokes and even petty vendettas, family members who have died often continue to relate to those who remain behind.

These true stories of ordinary men and women show that it is never too late to say the words left unspoken or to put right old wrongs. By doing this we can move forward, free to carry on with life in the reassuring knowledge that death is not always the end.

Cassandra Eason has collected case histories of mothers and children, grannies, uncles, aunties and lovers from all over the world who've called to say 'I love you' to those they've left behind.

# Embraced by the Light
## *What happens when you die?*

BETTY J. EADIE

Betty Eadie died after an operation, but was later to recover. It was during the intervening period of a few hours that she had what has been described by Raymond Moody as 'the most profound near-death experience ever'.

You will not fail to be moved by Betty's story. A devoted mother with a loving family, she embarked on a voyage of discovery, leaving her body and vising an afterworld of understanding, peace and joy. She was given a message to share with others that has filled hundreds of thousands of people with hope. *Embraced by the Light* recounts the people she met, the truths she learned and the magnificent realities of the spirit world. Her experiences changed her life forever. Reading this fascinating, dramatic and thought-provoking book may change yours too.

# Visions of Another World
## *The autobiograhy of a medium*

STEPHEN O'BRIEN

Phantom hands hammering on a door in the dead of night: THE SPIRIT WORLD WAS CALLING and Stephen O'Brien had to accept the remarkable powers which brought him *Visions of Another World*.

Then the tragic early death of his mother broke his life in two; but miraculously she appeared to him from beyond death and her love changed the course of his entire life: he became a medium and a visionary. He promised the soul of a long-dead Native American that he would serve the spirit world and countless thousands have packed out venues to hear him relate messages of Hope and Light from loved ones on the Other Side.

Over 30,000 of the so-called 'dead' have now communicated through Stephen O'Brien's amazing gifts, including war heroes, accident and murder victims, innocent children who died too young – even the world-famous actress Judy Garland. Now you can read Stephen O'Brien's touching and compelling story as he reveals to us all his *Visions of Another World*.

# Voices from Heaven
## *Communion with another world*

STEPHEN O'BRIEN

In the eagerly awaited sequel to his bestselling *Visions of Another World*, medium Stephen O'Brien shares with us more of his incredible adventures and psychic experiences. 'Death is an illusion,' says Stephen as he brings knowledge, love and hope from beyond the grave. He also includes startling messages from screen goddess Marilyn Monroe, Lord Olivier and even Lord Mountbatten of Burma.

In these fascinating recollections, Stephen crosses time zones and is transported back into previous centuries where he meets people who are long dead. He is also given glimpses of the future – among his many predictions he foresees the *Challenger* Space Shuttle disaster an incredible five years before it happened.

But the climax to this remarkable book is a unique set of journeys into the spirit world itself, revealing what awaits us all beyond death.

# The Essential Jesus
*Original sayings and earliest images*

JOHN DOMINIC CROSSAN

In his most concise and controversial portrait of Jesus yet, John Dominic Crossan reveals who Jesus really was prior to the New Testament Gospels and almost 2,000 years of Christian history.

Crossan's fresh translations of Jesus' sayings show him to be a teacher who lived his own radical message that all are equal before God. This picture is dramatically confirmed by the 30 earliest images of Jesus, which show that he was remembered by the first Christians not as God but as a revolutionary healer and leader.

# Mysterious Britain
## *A guide to ancient sites of Britain*

JANET AND COLIN BORD

* Why and how did ancient Britons transport huge bluestones over great distances to form their circles of standing stones?
* What is the truth about leys – the invisible straight lines connecting ancient sacred sites?
* For what purpose were earth mounds raised all over Britain and why did early Christians build their churches upon them?

The landscapes of Britain and Ireland are covered with ancient sites. Many places have mysteries and legends associated with them. Janet and Colin Bord have created a guide to both the sites and folklore of the two lands which includes standing stones, hill figures, holy wells and many other mysteries, from the Glastonbury Zodiac to the Marshfield Mummers.

'It is a fascinating and beautifully produced book, a kind of science fiction that looks into the past while suggesting some startling research for the future.' – *Evening News*

# Beneath the Wings of Angels
## *Autobiography of a medium*

BILLY ROBERTS WITH FIONA ROBERTS

Billy Roberts is a medium who has been to the gates of death many times, returning on each occasion with a message of hope and love. Born with extraordinary psychic gifts, he has survived extreme bad health to become one of the most remarkable and unconventional mediums in Britain.

This book is a down-to-earth and often humorous account of Billy's life. Born into a Liverpool family that was familiar with psychic phenomena, Billy's encounters with the spirit world started at a very early age, guiding him through his years as a rock musician and helping him to emerge from drug addiction. Eventually he accepted the reality of his gifts and became a working medium.

Through his work as teacher, healer and medium, Billy has helped many other people find their own courage and inspiration.

# Death: The Trip of a Lifetime

GREG PALMER

This is one man's attempt to understand the ultimate mystery. Anxious, slightly overweight and hitting middle age, Greg Palmer trudges around the world in his quest to find out how human culture, in all its diversity, responds to the universal experience of death. Full of much insight, humour and poignancy, Palmer's reflective narrative is an amazing and remarkably entertaining sort of travelogue.

From an examination of our fear and fascination with death, a look at both the physiological and psychological experience of death, and a cross-cultural display of funeral rites to an inquiry into the concept of the afterlife – via a London hospice, a death theme park in Taiwan, laser-show funerals in Japan and much more – *Death: The Trip of a Lifetime* comes to acknowledge death with humour, awe, respect and hope.

# In Tune with the Infinite
*Fullness of peace, power and plenty*

RALPH WALDO TRINE

'The optimist is right. The pessimist is right. The one differs from the other as the light from the dark. Yet both are right. Each is right from his own particular point of view, and this point of view is the determining factor in the life of each. It determines as to whether it is a life of power or of impotence, of peace or of pain, of success or of failure.'

So begins this remarkable seminal book, which has sold over 1,250,000 copies and has stood the test of time for nearly a century.

In its pages we find perennial truths that have been restated in many other forms in recent years, though perhaps never so clearly. By recognizing the power of our thought and by harmonizing our own with the Divine will, we will attract perfect peace, health, love, prosperity and success.

| | | | |
|---|---|---|---|
| FAMILIES ARE FOREVER | 1 85538 259 8 | £5.99 | ☐ |
| EMBRACED BY THE LIGHT | 1 85538 411 6 | £9.99 | ☐ |
| VISIONS OF ANOTHER WORLD | 0 85030 836 4 | £3.99 | ☐ |
| VOICES FROM HEAVEN | 1 85538 078 1 | £5.99 | ☐ |
| THE ESSENTIAL JESUS | 0 06 251044 4 | £12.90 | ☐ |
| MYSTERIOUS BRITAIN | 1 85538 461 2 | £8.99 | ☐ |
| BENEATH THE WINGS OF ANGELS | 1 85538 481 7 | £4.99 | ☐ |
| DEATH: THE TRIP OF A LIFETIME | 0 06 250803 2 | £8.99 | ☐ |
| IN TUNE WITH THE INFINITE | 1 85538 364 0 | £6.99 | ☐ |

All these books are available from your local bookseller or can be ordered direct from the publishers.

To order direct just tick the titles you want and fill in the form below:

Name: _____

Address: _____

_____

_____ Postcode: _____

Send to: Thorsons Mail Order, Dept 3, HarperCollins*Publishers*, Westerhill Road, Bishopbriggs, Glasgow G64 2QT.
Please enclose a cheque or postal order or your authority to debit your Visa/Access account –

Credit card no: _____

Expiry date: _____

Signature: _____

– to the value of the cover price plus:
**UK & BFPO:** Add £1.00 for the first book and 25p for each additional book ordered.
**Overseas orders including Eire:** Please add £2.95 service charge. Books will be sent by surface mail but quotes for airmail despatches will be given on request.

**24 HOUR TELEPHONE ORDERING SERVICE** FOR ACCESS/VISA CARDHOLDERS – TEL: 0141 772 2281.